TRANSFORMATION

Consciously Creating your Reality

CHOYO GOMEX

ISBN:

979-8348193935 (Paperback)

979-8348193959 (Hardcover)

TABLE OF CONTENTS

PROLOGUE

This ostensibly modest book is a treasure trove of metaphysical dynamite—immense wisdom that has the power to transform lives. It contains knowledge capable of unlocking profound personal growth and spiritual awakening for anyone who thoughtfully applies its techniques. Though the concepts may appear simple, they are rooted in ancient traditions steeped in the mystical insights of sages and spiritual guides from across centuries. For millennia, this wisdom has been carefully guarded and passed down, hidden in plain sight, known only to a select few who recognized its immense potential to change lives, societies, and even the course of history. The potential impact of this book on personal and collective transformation is profound, offering hope and inspiration in these tumultuous times.

Today, we stand at a critical juncture where humanity desperately needs such wisdom. The world is undergoing rapid and tumultuous change, shrouded in uncertainty and upheaval.   As the systems we rely on falter, there is a pressing need for teachings to guide us through these turbulent times with clarity, purpose, and compassion. It is often said, "When the house is on fire, valuable objects are thrown out of the window, regardless of what may happen to them, in the hope of saving something." This book is one of those invaluable objects— a gift to all ready to seize it in this pivotal moment. The urgency of our times demands action, and the knowledge within these pages offers a path to personal and collective transformation.

These teachings are not to be taken lightly. They demand a foundation of goodwill, integrity, and a genuine desire to uplift both yourself and those around you. In a world often dominated by self-interest and the pursuit of material gain, the principles outlined in this work provide a counterbalance—a path to creating a reality that benefits the individual and the collective. The power to manifest your desires and shape your reality is extraordinary, but with this power comes great responsibility. As you engage with the practices shared here, remember the crucial reminder found in the final chapter: *"Always ensure that your predominant desire is worthy and does not harm others, but rather brings benefit to you and everyone involved."*

We have all witnessed individuals who, armed with valuable knowledge, have used it solely for their own advantage, sometimes with harmful or unethical results. This is not the path this book encourages. It calls for a balanced approach that combines the strength of purpose with the wisdom and compassion of a generous heart. Just as King Solomon, revered for his knowledge, ruled with both might and kindness, so too must you wield the creative power within you responsibly and with love.

In ***TRANSFORMATION: Consciously Creating Your Reality***, I speak directly to you, dear reader, as a guide and a companion on this sacred journey of self-discovery and empowerment. Through the following pages, you will explore powerful tools and techniques designed to help you take control of your destiny and consciously and deliberately manifest the life you desire. This is not a passive read—it is an invitation to actively participate in your transformation, to align your thoughts, actions, and intentions with the life you seek to create.

I have chosen to write using feminine language to honor and celebrate the divine feminine energy that exists in all human beings.

This energy, often undervalued or ignored, is a crucial force of creation, nurturing, and transformation. And it plays an essential role in consciously shaping your reality. Regardless of gender, you are invited to embrace this energy as part of the transformational process.

This book is a powerful tool for those ready to make a shift and who are prepared to leave behind the limitations of their current existence and step into a new reality of their creation. Whether you are reading this or listening to the audio version, you are embarking on a journey that has the potential to transform not just your life but the world around you. Your reality is a canvas, and with conscious awareness, you can become the artist of your existence.

Enjoy the journey—one of creation, empowerment, and profound transformation.

INTRODUCTION

Weaving the Tapestry of Your Existence

At the heart of existence pulses an unimaginable power—a force that ancient sages intuited and that modern science is only now beginning to decipher. It's a force that transcends time and space, weaving together every atom, every thought, every experience in the grand tapestry of life. At the center of this force lies a profound truth: humans are not passive observers in the unfolding of their lives; we are active participants, capable of shaping our reality. Once fully grasped, this truth can transform how we live, love, and interact with the world around us.

TRANSFORMATION: *Consciously Creating Your Reality* is more than a mere book. It is a beacon illuminating the profound discovery that we can co-create our destiny. This is not just a collection of theories or abstract philosophies—it is a guide, a mentor, a companion on your journey to mastering the art and science of conscious creation. You are about to embark on a transformative adventure, one that will empower you to step into your full potential as the architect of your existence.

Have you ever stood under the vast night sky, gazing at the stars, and wondered about your place in this immense universe? Have you felt, deep within your soul, that there is something more—something beyond the tangible and the visible—that connects you to the very fabric of the cosmos? This feeling, this stirring within, is the voice of an ancient truth echoing through the ages: beyond the physical world we see, beyond the laws we understand, there is a subtler, more potent force at work, a force that binds together the threads of reality itself.

This book will explore the intersection of ancient wisdom and modern science, where timeless spiritual teachings meet the latest quantum physics and neuroscience discoveries. This intersection is where the secrets of consciously creating your reality unfold. We will journey from the depths of your inner world to the farthest reaches of the cosmos, uncovering how your thoughts, emotions, and actions shape your experiences.

This is not merely a bold assertion but an invitation to awaken your creative power. Your thoughts, emotions, and actions are not passive participants in the grand drama of life. Instead, they are the threads with which you weave the tapestry of your existence. With the proper understanding, intention, and action, you can shape these threads into a life that is not only meaningful but deeply fulfilling—a life that resonates with your highest aspirations and deepest desires.

Throughout the pages of this book, you will discover a vast array of tools and insights that will help you become a conscious creator of your reality. We will delve into both the art and the science of this process. You will learn how the spiritual teachings of ancient cultures, combined with groundbreaking modern scientific research, offer us a practical roadmap for shaping our personal universe. This book will provide the tools, guidance, and inspiration you need to take control of your destiny and bring your dreams to life.

At the heart of this journey are the stories of individuals who have harnessed the power of conscious creation to transform their lives. These aren't merely abstract theories—they are living, breathing examples of what is possible when you align your thoughts, emotions, and actions with the deeper currents of the universe. By mastering the art of conscious creation, you will meet people who have overcome adversity, achieved their dreams, and stepped into lives filled with purpose, joy, and abundance.

But this book is not just about inspiration—it is about empowerment. You will learn practical techniques and exercises you can apply daily, designed to help you move from theory to practice, from knowledge to mastery. These exercises are not simply rituals or affirmations—they are tools for transformation, rooted in both spiritual wisdom and scientific principles. Each exercise will bring you closer to mastering the process of conscious creation, enabling you to shape your inner world and the outer circumstances of your life.

You will see the world differently as you explore these ideas and practices. You will understand that you are not a victim of circumstance but the architect of your destiny. You will realize that you hold the brush with which to paint the canvas of your life, the pen with which to write your story. And with this realization comes a profound responsibility—to use your power wisely, with compassion, integrity, and a deep sense of purpose.

We live in a time of significant change, when humanity awakens to the truth of our creative potential. The old paradigms of victimhood, scarcity, and limitation are falling away, and a new paradigm is emerging—a paradigm in which we are active participants in the unfolding of our lives, co-creators with the universe in the manifestation of our deepest desires. This shift is not just a philosophical concept—it is a lived experience you are about to embark on.

In the following chapters, we will explore the cutting-edge discoveries in quantum physics, neuroscience, and psychology that reveal the profound interconnectedness of all things. We will see how these scientific insights mirror the teachings of ancient spiritual traditions, offering us a deeper understanding of how our thoughts and intentions shape the world around us. And most importantly, we will learn how to apply this knowledge practically to create the reality we desire consciously.

But knowledge alone is not enough. Transformation requires action. This book will provide you with insights and understanding and guide you through the practical steps necessary to bring your dreams into reality. Whether it is through meditation, visualization, or other powerful techniques, you will learn how to harness the power of your mind, emotions, and actions to create a life of abundance, joy, and fulfillment.

As you read these words, I invite you to open your mind to new possibilities. Challenge what you thought you knew about reality, destiny, and your ability to influence the course of your life. Embrace the idea that you are more powerful than you ever imagined and that the key to unlocking your full potential lies in the conscious, deliberate creation of your reality.

TRANSFORMATION: *Consciously Creating Your Reality* is not just a book—it is an invitation to step into a new way of living, a new paradigm of personal power and creative responsibility. It is a doorway into a future where you are the conscious creator of your life, where every thought, emotion, and action is an opportunity to shape the reality that reflects your highest self.

As you turn the pages of this book, you will learn how to create your reality at will and begin the process of doing so. You will embark on a journey of transformation that will continue long after the final page has been turned.

Welcome to the first day of the rest of your life. Welcome to the exact science and sublime art of consciously creating your reality. Welcome to a future of infinite possibilities.

CHAPTER I

The Law of Consciousness

In this world, a few individuals seem to have unlocked a secret—a power that allows them to rise above the masses and live lives filled with success, joy, and fulfillment. This power is a mystery to many, something others dismiss as mere "luck." Perhaps you, too, believe that some people are born under a lucky star, blessed with opportunities that the rest of us can only dream of. But what if I told you that this assumption, this belief in luck as the governing force in life, is missing something critical? What if I told you that the key to success and happiness lies not in luck but in something far more profound and accessible to every person on this planet?

This book is written for those willing to entertain the possibility that life's outcomes—both its triumphs and its failures—are governed by something far more significant than random chance. There is a law at work in the universe that many are unaware of, but it holds the answers to the disparities between happiness and sorrow, success and failure. This is the Law of Consciousness. It is a principle that offers an effective method for addressing the challenges and dilemmas of life, a method that has been successfully employed by thousands of people—people of average means and abilities—who have transformed their lives through its use. Many who have benefited from this law were unaware they were using it, but ignorance does not diminish its effectiveness.

As the saying goes, "Seek, and you shall find." If you are seeking answers and are willing to open your mind to new possibilities, then what you find within these pages could change your life. But remember, possessing knowledge alone is not enough. Your life will not change simply because you read this book. It will only change when you apply what you learn. I can offer you the key to this transformative knowledge, but you must open the door. No one else can do it for you, and waiting for someone or something external—a "superhero" or a stroke of good fortune—is a futile endeavor. True power lies within you.

Understanding the Visible and the Invisible

Let's start by grounding ourselves in some fundamental, observable facts about the world. When you look around, what do you see? A world full of objects: houses, trees, people, and countless other forms. These objects appear distinct, with their own characteristics like color, texture, density, and weight. But if you look deeper, you'll find that all these objects, though different on the surface, share a common essence. Everything in your environment is made of matter, and matter is visible to the naked eye. But not everything that shapes your reality is visible.

Have you ever watched an apple fall from a tree? You see the apple, which moves, but you don't see the force that causes it to fall. This invisible force, gravity, is genuine, even though it cannot be directly observed. Similarly, we experience other forces like electricity, magnetism, and wind, none of which are visible but all of which profoundly affect the world around us. We don't see the wind, but we feel it. We don't see electricity powering our devices but rely on it daily. Though unseen, these invisible forces drive the phenomena we observe.

The same principle applies to the human mind. No one has ever seen the mind itself, yet no one doubts its existence. The mind, though invisible, is the most powerful force you possess. Everything humans have ever created—from skyscrapers to symphonies—originated as a thought in the mind. Before your house was built, it was an idea in the architect's mind. Before your car rolled off the assembly line, it was conceived in the mind of an engineer. Every human accomplishment, every material creation, began with a thought. The invisible power of thought gave rise to the visible form.

Now, consider the natural world. Humans can create houses, cars, and technologies, but they cannot create a tree, an ocean, or a bird. These things existed long before human ingenuity could explain them, and they, too, began in the mind. But whose mind? What force conceived the mountains, the forests, and the creatures that fill our world? Before addressing this question, let's take a closer look at the concept of human-made and natural growth.

The Two Types of Growth

Look around and notice two distinct types of growth happening all around you. On the one hand, you observe the development of human-made structures—buildings, bridges, and roads. These structures rise due to human effort, guided by the blueprints created in human minds. A building that started construction a few weeks ago grows taller with each passing day as workers labor to bring the architect's vision into reality. A subway system that began months ago is now nearing completion. Human hands and human ingenuity drive this growth.

On the other hand, we observe growth in the natural world. The tree that was small last year is now taller. The child who was once an infant has grown in size and skill. The seasons change, the plants grow, and the animals live and reproduce. This type of growth happens without direct human intervention. An invisible force guides it—call it nature, call it life—propelling living things to grow, develop, and thrive.

So, are these two types of growth—human-made and natural— genuinely separate? At first glance, they seem different. But when we delve deeper, we see they are expressions of the same underlying principle. Just as human-made structures begin as thoughts in a human mind, so too do natural forms begin as thoughts in the mind of the universe, or what some call the Universal Mind. This Universal Mind is the same force that creates the oceans, the mountains, and the forests, and it is the same force that gives rise to human thought and creation.

The Universal Mind and the Great Cause

No rational person would argue that humans appeared out of nowhere. We, too, are part of this grand web of creation, brought into existence by the same force that governs the rest of the universe. But what is this force? Throughout history, humans have called it God, Spirit, the Great First Cause. Regardless of our name, the essential truth remains the same—there is an unseen intelligence, a Universal Mind, that governs everything in existence.

This Universal Mind is the source of all power and creation. It is the invisible force behind the visible world. Its intelligence gives rise to both natural and human-made phenomena.

It is the power that flows through you and me, guiding our thoughts, actions, and creations. We can shape our reality through our connection to this Universal Mind.

Though some may associate the idea of a Universal Mind with religion or theology, it is a concept grounded in spiritual traditions and modern science. Quantum physics, for example, tells us that everything in the universe is interconnected and that at the most fundamental level, everything is made of energy. This energy is not random—it is organized, structured, and governed by laws that we are only beginning to understand.

The Universal Mind is the intelligence that governs these laws, and it operates through our consciousness. This is where the Law of Consciousness comes into play. Just as the physical universe operates according to laws like gravity and electromagnetism, so too does the mental and spiritual realm operate according to the Law of Consciousness. This law states that your thoughts and beliefs shape your reality. What you hold in your mind, you manifest in your life.

The Power of Thought

Understanding the Law of Consciousness is the key to unlocking the power within you. Everything in your life—your circumstances, your relationships, your successes and failures—is a reflection of your inner world. The thoughts, beliefs, and emotions you cultivate create the conditions of your external reality. This is not just a metaphor; it is a literal truth. Your thoughts are powerful forces, shaping the fabric of your existence just as gravity shapes the planets' movement.

The challenge, of course, is learning to consciously direct your thoughts in a way that aligns with your desires. Most people live their lives unconsciously, reacting to the world around them rather than actively creating it. They are like ships adrift at sea, tossed about by the waves of circumstance, unaware that they hold the power to steer their course. But when you understand the Law of Consciousness, you realize you are not at the mercy of external events. You are the captain of your ship, capable of charting a course toward the life you truly desire.

This journey begins with a simple but profound realization: **what you think you will become**. Your dominant thoughts, beliefs, and feelings are constantly shaping your reality. If you believe that you are unlucky, that life is hard, and that success is out of reach, then that is what you will experience. But if you believe you are a powerful creator capable of manifesting your desires, then that is the reality you will begin to experience.

As you delve deeper into this book, you will discover practical techniques for harnessing the power of your thoughts and aligning them with the Universal Mind. These techniques are not mystical or esoteric but rooted in ancient wisdom and modern science. Learning to direct your thoughts consciously can transform your life from the inside out.

Conclusion: Awakening to Your Power

The journey ahead will take you beyond the surface of everyday life and into the deeper realms of consciousness, where the true power to shape your reality resides.

You will learn how to align your thoughts and actions with the Universal Mind, enabling you to create the life you desire consciously. This is not a passive process—it requires active engagement, practice, and a willingness to question old beliefs and habits. As you understand your consciousness's role in shaping your reality, you will awaken to a more profound truth: the power to create the life you want has always been within you.

But awakening to this power is only the beginning. Once you realize your thoughts, beliefs, and emotions' profound impact on your world, the real work begins. The Law of Consciousness is neither a quick fix nor a magic solution to life's problems. It is a natural law, as unchanging as gravity, and like any law, it operates whether you are aware of it or not. Your thoughts will continue to shape your reality, whether you consciously direct them or let them run on autopilot. The difference lies in your awareness and ability to harness this law to your advantage.

This book is designed to guide you through awakening and mastery. Each chapter offers new insights and practical techniques to help you understand and apply the Law of Consciousness in your daily life. You will learn how to break free from limiting beliefs, cultivate empowering thoughts, and align your emotions and actions with your highest intentions. This journey is one of self-discovery, but it is also a journey of self-mastery.

As you apply the principles outlined in this book, you will notice changes in your life. At first, these changes may be subtle—perhaps a shift in your attitude, increased clarity, or a new sense of confidence. However, as you continue to practice these techniques over time, the changes will become more apparent. You will begin to see tangible results in your outer world reflecting the inner shifts within you. Opportunities will arise where none seemed possible before. Relationships will improve, and obstacles that once felt insurmountable will begin to dissolve.

Conscious creation is not always easy, requiring patience and persistence. There will be moments when doubt creeps in, old habits and beliefs resurface, and external circumstances challenge your newfound understanding. In those moments, it is crucial to remember that you are not a victim of your environment. You have the power to choose your thoughts, to direct your consciousness, and to create the reality you desire.

You will encounter setbacks and challenges throughout this journey, but these are not signs of failure. They are opportunities for growth, refining your understanding, and deepening your mastery of the Law of Consciousness. Each challenge is a stepping stone toward greater awareness and empowerment. As you continue to practice and apply these principles, you will become more adept at navigating the complexities of life with grace and ease. You will begin to see yourself not as a passive observer of your circumstances but as a conscious creator, capable of shaping your world according to your deepest desires and highest aspirations.

The ultimate goal of this journey is not merely to achieve external success or happiness, though these will naturally follow as you align yourself with the Universal Mind. The true purpose of this work is to awaken to your full potential as a creative being, to realize that you are an integral part of the infinite intelligence that governs the universe, and to live in harmony with this truth. When you fully embrace your role as a conscious creator, you step into a new way of being—one guided by wisdom, purpose, and a deep sense of connection to the greater whole.

As you read through the following chapters, remember that the power you seek is already within you. You do not need to acquire it from some external source, nor do you need to wait for the right moment to begin. The moment is now. The key to transforming your life lies in understanding and applying the Law of Consciousness, and the time to start is today.

You are about to embark on a journey of self-transformation that will empower you to take control of your life and shape your destiny with intention and purpose. The path ahead may sometimes be challenging, but the rewards are immeasurable. As you awaken to your true potential and create your reality consciously, you will experience a profound sense of fulfillment and joy that comes from living in alignment with your highest self.

The Law of Consciousness is not a secret reserved for a select few; it is a universal principle anyone can access and apply. It is the key to unlocking the life of your dreams, and it is available to you right now. All you need to do is decide to use it. You hold the power to create your reality; with that power comes the responsibility to shape it with care, wisdom, and love.

As we conclude this chapter, I invite you to reflect on the possibilities before you. Imagine what your life could be like if you fully embraced your role as a conscious creator. What would you create? How would you live? What kind of world would you build for yourself and others? These are not idle questions—they are the starting point of your journey toward transformation.

Remember, you are not alone on this path. Countless others have walked it before you, and many more will follow in your footsteps. The principles you are about to learn have been used by individuals throughout history to achieve extraordinary things, and they are just as powerful and relevant today as ever. As you move forward, trust in the process and trust in yourself. You are capable of greatness, and your desired life is within reach.

The journey of conscious creation involves discovery, growth, and empowerment. It is a journey that will take you beyond the limitations of your current reality and into a future of infinite possibilities. As you step into this new way of being, you will understand that there are no limits to what you can achieve and no barriers to the life you can create. The power of the Universal Mind is within you, and with it, you can transform your world.

Welcome to the beginning of a new chapter in your life. Welcome to the journey of consciously creating your reality. The adventure begins now.

CHAPTER II
Unity in Diversity

L et's explore that "magical something" that allows some people to succeed beyond their apparent abilities. Remember, we only see the effects of their actions but not the skills that enable them to do so.

Perhaps those we have envied or called "lucky" have learned a great truth, which begins to unfold before us as we study the invisible causes of visible effects. We understand that all these invisible causes focus on the action of the Universal Mind, of which our minds are its expression. We also see that our minds operate in two ways: objective and subjective. Our objective mind can influence each of us' subjective minds. The sole mission of the subjective mind is to carry out orders automatically and decisively, without any will of its own.

We know that the conscious mind can influence processes typically managed by the unconscious mind, such as breathing, circulation, and digestion. However, if this influence were limited only to such automatic functions, we would rarely need to control them consciously. So, don't you think it would be wise to seek some more important reason for the potential control of the conscious mind?

It should be clear that nature does not uselessly develop faculties and talents. This point relies on the absolute unity of all things with the Universal Mind, regardless of their apparent physical separation.

This idea is so essential to understanding our topic better that we will dedicate a bit more time to it now so that it is evident in our consciousness how this can be and why it is what it is.

I do not intend to complicate this or lead you through a maze of metaphysics in this search. So, we will take a couple of simple illustrations that will clearly explain this idea of unity and the absolute need for you to understand it truly.

Are you familiar with bicycle wheels? Have you ever thought of it as a beautiful symbol of cosmic truth? Probably not, because we usually don't observe the symbols in everyday items.

A bicycle wheel has a hub, spokes, rim, and tire. Now, imagine that the hub represents the Universal Mind. Let each gear on the wheel represent a human being, a race, or a nation. Let's call this wheel the cycle of human existence. Let the teeth on the rim represent individual life incidents and experiences.

First, to capture our attention, we have the fact that all the wheel spokes originate from a common center—the Universal Mind. Then we see that from that common center of origin, each contact is part of the central axis. Similarly, in the Universal Mind, all human beings, races, and nations are ONE and part of each other.

But when each spoke of the wheel moves outward—toward the cycle of life—it seems to separate, and by the time it reaches the edge, it feels alone and distant from its neighbor. I say "apparently separated," but in reality, each spoke is connected at the hub and is part of the whole wheel.

However, as human beings in the wheel of life, the mistaken idea still prevails that we are separated and that individuality means being different. This is where human error begins because people ignore the fact that a coherent and united nation would be mighty.

An individual who thinks they are the law unto themselves will fail miserably because they will have lost their strength by not understanding the essential value of unity and that everything in nature contains all the powers of nature itself. And that everything in the Universe is made of the same substance.

Perhaps human beings think of themselves as separate from the human brotherhood and feel abandoned, neglected, discriminated against, and burdened with a disproportionate load. But this is not so, for they are simply carrying their burden, in their own time, in exact obedience to a law that says: "Each will carry only what is rightfully theirs."

Please take a deep breath and seriously meditate on this information before proceeding.

It's not about finishing the book quickly. If you genuinely wish to change and improve your life, I suggest you use all your power of understanding to become aware of the unity and connection of all seemingly separate events and things.

Now, take a piece of paper, make five holes in it, and insert each of the five fingers of one of your hands into the holes.

The five fingers protruding from the paper represent five separate things to someone standing before you. Each finger appears to have individual movement power and seems wholly independent and separate from its neighbor. But to you, behind the paper, "beyond the veil," so to speak, it is undeniable that all fingers are connected, have something in common, and derive their power from the same source—in this case, your hand.

Do you see this illustration?

For human beings, frustration and discouragement from feeling separate can be overwhelming, especially when we perceive the world as chaotic and disorderly. When we feel trapped, with no visible way out or support within reach, our ability to face challenges diminishes significantly. This reduction in our ability, power, vitality, strength, and energy is primarily due to a negative perception of our situation.

It's common for many frustrated people to wrongly believe they have been isolated from their sources of power and vital energy, intensifying helplessness, overwhelm, and limitation. Recognizing this mistaken perception is the first step toward recovering our inner strength and reconnecting with our source of resilience and hope.

Now I want to personalize this: When you feel frustrated and discouraged, which can sometimes be overwhelming, especially when you perceive the world as chaotic and without order when you feel trapped and without an apparent solution to your dilemmas, your ability to think clearly and face challenges diminishes significantly. This decrease in your ability, power, vitality, strength, and energy is mainly due to a negative perception of your situation. In those moments, it's common to mistakenly believe that you have been isolated and separated from your source of power and vital energy, intensifying the feeling of helplessness and limitation. Recognizing this mistaken perception is the first step toward recovering your inner strength and reconnecting with your source of power, resilience, and hope.

So, when you feel alone, frustrated, stressed, despised, and abandoned, remember that we are all ONE with the creative source, with our Creator, that we are One in the Universal Mind, we are ONE with all the creative force of nature; recognize that you can never truly be "alone." Acknowledge with certainty that you are a creator goddess and possess the same creative power of the universal mind, but only to a different degree. This power within you is patiently waiting to be used. When you learn how to use it, manifesting anything, any desire, will seem like child's play.

By now, it should be clear to you that to have things you've never had, you must start doing things you've never done and know that your mission now is to recognize and rearrange the things that no longer work, serve, or help in your life. You must consciously harmonize and align your vibration, your vital energy, with everything in the Universal Mind. Doing this will give you access to powers you never imagined were available.

Please, stop now and seriously meditate on this; don't continue reading until you consciously accept this fact—this is how important it is.

At this point, we could say we are just beginning this informative journey; more valuable information is yet to come. That's why this foundation must be well-established and transparent. I recommend reading this book several times, as many times as necessary.

Later, we will delve into the specific details of how you can use this power for yourself, for your benefit, and the benefit of others involved. But remember, just having the information—just "knowing it"—will be useless to you. It's in the application of the information that its value resides.

So, let's continue. Now think about this: If you go to a large power plant, you'll observe its great dynamo and astounding power. The dynamo is ready to do its job when activated simply by moving the switch button. If no one turns it on, that great dynamo will do nothing until the demand for its energy is required. But the moment it is activated, by turning on the switch, the energy flows through its cables. It's clear then that the dynamo must first be activated before it begins to exert its power.

But if you don't know that the dynamo exists or don't believe it—even after being told so many times—what's the point of me telling you how to use it? Do you see what I mean?

That's why I'm now interested in telling you how to apply this information to yourself. It's crucial that you know you already have a dynamo within you, and in fact, you were born with it. Your dynamo is millions of times more powerful than all the most powerful dynamos created by humans combined. You must know that this power source already exists within you, and just like the dynamo in a power plant, your dynamo is merely waiting for you to switch it on, to activate it, so it can start working, to convert all your desires into reality. But no external entity will come to help you or do the things you want until you recognize its existence, activate it, and direct it yourself toward your desired goal.

I'm talking to you about the greatest power in the world, much more significant than any dynamo invented by humans, because it's the power that enabled humans to invent the dynamo, among many other things.

I'll tell you something: there is a certain way of doing things, and once you understand this way, you can make that power work for you.

Ready for what's coming? Fasten your seatbelt because this journey is just beginning.

The Lighthouse That Guides Your Actions

To grasp the concepts, I'll explain them better and more effectively, it's first necessary to understand how they work. Picture your mind as a house that, over time, has been filled with unnecessary things. Although it might appear orderly outside, the interior could be in chaos. To achieve success, cleaning the house is crucial, leaving only the essentials.

The transformation you seek—physical, mental, and emotional—requires an internal cleansing. Just as a cluttered house makes it difficult to find what you need, a cluttered mind prevents you from reaching your full potential. We must free our minds from limiting beliefs and useless thoughts that hold us back.

Think about how you became who you are. You started as a tiny cell that could fit on the tip of a pin, yet it already contained everything you are now. That cell, driven by a spark of mind, followed a divine plan, developing into the person you are. Even if you don't fully understand this truth, you can recognize that there was a creative power at work.

This principle is the foundation of this teaching: the mind contains images, and each image will eventually manifest on the physical plane. This is the Universal Law, which, when used intelligently, gives us control over our environment. The mind is a powerful tool for transformation. If we focus our thoughts on what we truly desire, we can materialize those desires in our physical, mental, and emotional reality.

Surprisingly, you've likely experienced "coincidences" where something you wanted appeared. This is not mere chance but the result of this law. However, many desires don't manifest due to a lack of attention or ignorance of this law. Imagine if all radio stations broadcasted on the same frequency. It would be impossible to hear a single station.

In the same way, our thoughts and desires can become confused and cancel each other out, preventing their manifestation.

The power of the mind weakens when we believe that external forces are more powerful than our mind. The mental image you hold is the thing itself, and what you experience through your senses is that image manifested. Understanding and applying this principle is essential for any personal transformation process.

Consider how science tells us that the human body renews completely every eleven months. If that's true, and it is, how can we maintain memories from our childhood if our cells are only eleven months old? We are not just the body; we are the mind, a unique entity that uses the body to express thoughts and ideas. Physical transformation, therefore, is not just a superficial change; it's intimately connected with mental and emotional transformation.

Our mind is like a garden. Cultivating it with positive and constructive thoughts will improve physical and emotional well-being. Neglecting it will fill us with weeds—negative thoughts and limiting beliefs—that will choke our growth.

True transformation starts in the mind, and its effects are reflected in our bodies and emotions.

Although it may seem like we have three minds, there are actually three phases of the same mind: the deep mind, which controls the body's functions; the conscious mind, which interacts with the external world; and the subconscious mind, which is the center of power within us. The subconscious mind is powerful, but it depends on the conscious mind to receive instructions.

Why don't we all live extraordinary lives if we all possess a powerful subconscious mind? Because the conscious mind, upon receiving information from the five senses, often judges and limits itself, diverting the energy of the subconscious mind towards new objectives without allowing it to complete its work. It's like trying to transform your body, but every time you start a new exercise routine, you change your mind and try something else without giving your body time to adapt and show results. The same happens with the mind.

The key to activating the power of the subconscious mind is to maintain a clear and defined goal. Just like a plane constantly corrects its course but always heads towards its destination, we must have a clear image of what we want to achieve and not give up until we get it. This is fundamental to transformation in all its forms.

Having a well-defined goal is essential for several reasons.

First, the subconscious mind is the positive pole of your being, while the conscious mind is the negative pole. For something to manifest, there must be a balance between both poles.

Second, the atmosphere is full of millions of thoughts in motion. If you don't have a clear goal, you'll be at the mercy of those conflicting ideas, leading to confusion and frustration.

Finally, when you focus on a specific desire, you transfer some of your creative energy to that goal. But if you simultaneously scatter that energy across many desires, your power is diluted, and you achieve little. This is a crucial principle for your transformation. If you want physical, mental, or emotional change, you must concentrate on that specific goal until it is realized.

Suppose your goal is to improve your physical health. If you dedicate yourself to an exercise plan with determination and consistency, your body will transform. However, progress will be slow or nonexistent if you constantly change your routine or get distracted by other goals. The same goes for the mind. To develop a more positive mindset, you must focus on it daily, feeding your mind with thoughts reinforcing that transformation. Emotional transformation follows this pattern, too: it requires focus, consistency, and a clear vision of what you want to achieve.

If your significant goal requires many small steps, focus on one at a time. Complete each task before moving on to the next. This way, you'll avoid feeling overwhelmed and ensure steady progress toward your goal. Patience and consistency are key in this process. With time and dedication, you can transform your dreams into reality.

Or if your goal is to achieve mental and emotional peace. You know this goal won't be achieved overnight but through small steps: daily meditation, gratitude practices, and eliminating negative thoughts. Every step is essential and contributes to the result. The same applies to physical transformation: every workout, every healthy meal, and every hour of rest are building blocks that lead to the desired change.

Transformation is an ongoing process that encompasses body, mind, and emotions. It's not enough to change just one aspect; working on all levels is necessary for true and lasting transformation. Your mind is the guide, the lighthouse that illuminates the path to change. By disciplining your conscious mind and aligning your thoughts with your deepest desires, you can activate the power of your subconscious mind to manifest any transformation you desire.

Remember that transformation is not a destination but a journey that requires clarity, focus, and determination. By maintaining a clear vision of your goal and moving towards it with deliberate steps, you'll create a new you and reality in which your most profound desires become tangible. Such is the power of your mind, and it's at your disposal to use in your transformation process.

On this journey, every small action counts. Everything contributes to the person you are becoming; from the thoughts you choose to your decisions. Physical, mental, and emotional transformation does not happen overnight but results from a constant commitment to personal growth. If you stay focused on your goals and persevere, the transformation will be inevitable and profound.

CHAPTER III

The Link That Connects Everything

If you've been following closely up until now, you should have these core concepts clearly understood:

❖ **Everything is ONE in the Universal Mind.**

❖ **You are a unique channel for expressing that creative Universal Mind.**

❖ **In your human experience, you use objective and subjective minds.**

❖ **Your conscious mind can influence your unconscious mind, acting on your commands.**

❖ **While the unconscious mind typically governs automatic bodily functions, it can also act on other activities directed by your conscious mind.**

Does this sound familiar? If so, that's excellent. Let's move forward and explore a new dimension of this relationship. We've established the significance of the Universal Mind, and now we must delve into how this power, operating through your subjective mind, can connect everything in your reality. But how exactly can your subjective mind take orders beyond automatic bodily functions?

The Power of the Subjective Mind

To understand this better, let's consider a well-known phenomenon: **hypnosis**. Imagine a hypnotist in action, controlling a volunteer's behavior on stage. With just a few gestures, the hypnotist puts the person into a trance, disconnecting their conscious mind and gaining control over their unconscious mind. What does this mean? Essentially, the hypnotist's conscious mind has temporarily taken control of the subject's unconscious mind.

In this trance state, the subject has no memory of what occurs. Their unconscious mind, which typically controls their body's automatic functions, is now entirely under the hypnotist's direction. The subject might be asked to bark like a dog, run around the stage, or perform other acts—seemingly absurd but carried out without hesitation. The **unconscious mind** doesn't question these commands; it simply accepts them and acts on them automatically. The hypnotist proves that the **subjective mind** can be influenced to perform extraordinary tasks without asking.

This demonstrates an essential fact: if someone else can impress their will upon your subconscious mind, then **you can do the same**— and more efficiently—by directing your subconscious mind with your **conscious mind**. Hypnosis is just one extreme example, but it shows how responsive and impressionable the subjective mind can be.

The Universal Nature of the Subconscious

One of the most fascinating aspects of the subconscious mind is that it can **interact with others' conscious minds**.

Hypnosis works because the subject's subconscious mind cannot distinguish between their conscious mind and the hypnotist's. It simply follows its commands, making the unconscious mind **impersonal** and universal in its reactions.

Unlike the conscious mind, which carefully analyzes, discriminates, and evaluates, the **subconscious mind** does not discriminate. It doesn't debate reasons or consider the pros and cons. It is, in essence, **universal**, reacting in the same way regardless of the source of the command. Your **conscious mind**, by contrast, is **specific**. It processes information based on individual experiences, analyzing each detail to make decisions in the physical world.

Understanding this distinction between the conscious and subconscious minds is critical to mastering the art of using your mind effectively. Your conscious mind navigates the external, physical world, while your subconscious mind connects to the Universal Mind, a force far beyond the limits of physical reality.

The Subconscious Mind is the Link to the Universal Mind

Now that we know the subconscious mind is universal in nature, we arrive at an important realization: **your subconscious mind is your immediate, personal link to the Universal Mind**. You can access the vast creative force that underpins everything through this connection.

It's crucial to understand that while humans cannot directly communicate with the Universal Mind on a conscious level, they don't need to. The subconscious mind mediates, linking individual consciousness with the infinite Universal Mind. This connection is the key to everything. When you learn to communicate with your subconscious, you gain access to the power to transform your thoughts into reality.

The **Universal Mind** expresses itself through the human mind, and the human mind can only express itself through the Universal Mind. The two are intertwined, **one and the same**. Therefore, learning how to communicate with your subconscious mind is like possessing the keys to the kingdom—unlocking the door to infinite possibilities.

Communicating with the Subconscious Mind

So, how can we communicate effectively with the subconscious mind? The process begins with two fundamental elements: **imagination** and **silence**. All creation starts in the imagination, and all answers can be found in the silence.

To access the subconscious, the conscious mind must first **relax**. This can be achieved through practices such as **meditation**. By quieting the conscious mind, you create space for the subconscious to emerge, enabling a direct line of communication between your conscious desires and the Universal Mind.

Consider the biblical passage from Matthew 18:19: "When two are in agreement about any one thing on earth and ask for it, the Heavenly Father will grant it to them." This concept is powerful, yet few people understand who those "two" are.

The answer lies in the alignment between your **conscious and subconscious minds**. When these two aspects of your mind agree, you can manifest anything you desire.

In Matthew 7:7-12, another profound truth is revealed: "Ask, and it will be given to you; seek, and you will find; knock, and it will be opened to you." The method for asking, seeking, and knocking is what we will now explore. The key to success is using the **subconscious mind** to manifest your desires.

The Manifestation Process

To manifest your desires, follow this step-by-step process:

1.   **Desire:** The process begins with a burning desire for something specific. The desire must be clear and strong.
2.   **Acceptance:** You must **accept** that this desire is achievable and within your power to manifest.

Once these two elements are established, you can focus on the desired outcome. Here's how:

- **Relaxation:** Sit in silence, take deep breaths, and consciously relax your body. Allow your mind to become still.
- **Visualization:** Begin to imagine what you desire vividly. Picture it in as much detail as possible. Use all five senses—see the colors, hear the sounds, feel the textures, and even taste and smell elements of the scene. The more lifelike your visualization, the more powerfully it will impress the subconscious mind.

For example, if you desire a certain sum of money, imagine yourself already possessing it. Picture the money in your bank account or your hands. Visualize using it to buy something meaningful or pay off a debt. The more precise the image, the faster it will impress your subconscious mind.

3.   **Claiming:** After visualizing your desire, **claim it** as yours. Look into a mirror, speak your name, and declare your power to manifest this desire. Repeat affirmations that

reinforce your belief in your inherent creative power, such as: "I command the power within me to maintain this image until it becomes my reality."

4. **Emotional Connection:** It's essential to connect emotionally with the visualization. The subconscious mind responds not just to images but also to the **emotions** attached to those images. The stronger the emotional charge, the more powerful the impression on the subconscious.

Consistency and Patience

The manifestation process doesn't end with a single visualization session. You must **repeat** the process regularly, consistently reinforcing the image in your subconscious mind. This repetition helps the subconscious mind imprint the desired outcome into the Universal Mind, setting the manifestation process into motion.

It's important not to worry about the **how**—how your desire will manifest. That's not your concern. Your job is to focus on your desire with clarity and conviction, trusting that the Universal Mind will orchestrate the necessary circumstances to bring it into reality.

Belief and Conviction

Above all, you must believe in the power of your subconscious mind to bring your desires to life. You will hinder the manifestation if you doubt your worthiness or question the process. It would be best to fully embrace the certainty that what you desire is already on its way, that it is already a reality in the **universal realm** and will soon manifest in the **physical realm**.

Remember, **thoughts alone** are not enough. There must be a **strong motivating** force behind the thought. The emotion and belief attached to the thought give it power and ensure its realization. This is why some people seem to achieve their desires effortlessly, while others struggle—those who succeed have mastered the art of aligning thought, emotion, and belief.

Understanding Limitations

The subconscious mind, though powerful, operates within the limits of our physical reality. It cannot override the laws of nature—such as gravity or time—and therefore cannot perform impossible feats like making you fly or instantly grow taller. However, the subconscious mind can achieve extraordinary things within our world's natural laws. It can bring you health, success, and happiness if your desires do not conflict with the physical laws of time and space.

Conclusion: The Link to Everything

As we conclude this chapter, it's clear that the **subconscious mind** is your link to the **Universal Mind** and the **creative power** of the universe. By learning to communicate effectively with your subconscious, you can harness this power to manifest your material, emotional, or spiritual desires.

But before moving on, ensure you fully understand the concepts covered here. This chapter has laid the groundwork for mastering the connection between your **conscious**, **subconscious**, and the **Universal Mind**. Understanding these relationships is crucial because it allows you to tap into the infinite creative power that can shape your reality.

By now, you should recognize that your **subconscious mind** is the intermediary between your conscious thoughts and the Universal Mind's vast potential. This means you can use your conscious thoughts to plant seeds in your subconscious, manifesting those desires into your physical world, provided they align with natural laws. Strong emotions and beliefs support them.

So, here are the key takeaways to fully grasp before moving forward:

1. **Everything is connected through the Universal Mind**, and your subconscious is the link to it.
2. **You have the power to influence your subconscious mind**, which in turn can shape your reality.

3.   **Visualization, belief, and emotional conviction** are essential tools in impressing your desires onto your subconscious mind.

4.   **Repetition and patience** are crucial. Manifestation is not instantaneous, but with consistent focus and belief, your desires will come to fruition.

5.   **Limitation exists only in the realm of physical laws**, but your subconscious mind can accomplish what seems like miracles within those.

You are now equipped with the knowledge that **you are an individual expression of the Universal Mind**, and by aligning your conscious and subconscious minds, you can direct your life's course with clarity, purpose, and power. From here on, the only limits are those you set for yourself.

What's Next?

In the upcoming chapters, we will explore practical applications, strengthen our connection to the subconscious, and expand our ability to manifest our desires. But before proceeding, ensure you have fully absorbed the principles in this chapter. These foundational ideas will act as your compass, guiding you as you continue to discover the immense potential within you.

So, take the time to review, reflect, and apply what you've learned so far. Once you feel ready, you can move on to the next stage of your journey, where you will learn how to apply these principles to specific areas of your life—health, wealth, relationships, and personal fulfillment.

Remember, **you hold the key** to your own power; with it, you can unlock the reality you wish to create. The journey has only just begun, and what lies ahead is the limitless potential that comes with understanding and utilizing the **link that connects everything**.

CHAPTER IV

Seeing Beyond the Parts

Revisiting Core Principles

Before continuing this transformative journey, it's essential to reestablish the foundational principles guiding our exploration. These ideas are the bedrock of the reality you wish to create:

1. **Everything is interconnected.** All things governed by divine law are unified within the Universal Mind. The separations we perceive in life—between people, objects, and events—are illusions created by our senses.

2. **You are a unique expression of the Universal Mind**, operating on two levels: the external, conscious mind, "objective," and the internal, subconscious mind, "subjective."

3. **Experiences and judgments limit your objective mind**, but your subconscious mind, which controls all vital internal functions, has access to limitless power.

4. **Your conscious mind can influence the subconscious**, programming it to work for you. This process can activate forces far beyond the capabilities of your conscious mind alone.

Understanding these principles is not a mental exercise alone. Grasping them, opens the gateway to accessing powers that radically transform your life experience. If these ideas are clear, we can now dive deeper. If not, it's crucial to revisit them—because everything that follows is built upon this foundation.

Reversing the Process: Creating from Within

In previous chapters, we've discussed the relationship between your conscious and subconscious minds. Now, it's time to explore how the conscious mind can direct the subconscious to bring about your desired circumstances. This is a fundamental shift, a reversal of how you perceive reality.

Consider this: Most people passively observe the world around them, reacting to what their five senses present to them. They believe their reality is fixed and shaped by external forces. But what if you could reverse this dynamic? Instead of simply reacting to the world, what if you could intentionally create images of what you wish to experience and then watch them unfold in your physical reality?

Imagine the creative process like this: When you observe a painting, you take in the image with your eyes and recreate it in your imagination. The painting itself results from a prior creative act, a projection of someone's inner vision onto the canvas.

Now, reverse this process. Instead of reacting to what already exists, we consciously create the image of what we desire, impressing it upon our subconscious. The subconscious will, in turn, bring this image into reality.

This is the cornerstone of manifestation and Transformation

All creation begins in the imagination. The form that you give to your thoughts becomes the form that you experience in the external world.

The subconscious mind accepts the images and commands given to it by the conscious mind and works tirelessly to manifest them. It never questions or judges; it simply executes the orders it receives.

This process sounds simple but requires discipline, intention, and emotional involvement. You must vividly create the image of your desire in your mind's eye, with as much color, detail, and emotion as you can muster. This is the "seed" you plant in the fertile soil of your subconscious. From there, trust that the Universal Mind will handle the rest, and know that your role is to focus your conscious mind on the desired outcome while patiently awaiting its physical manifestation.

The Art of Visualization: More Than Just Imagery

We've discussed the importance of creating vivid mental images, but it's crucial to understand that **visualization is more than just seeing**. It's about immersing all your senses into the creative process. The more lifelike and multisensory your mental image, the more powerfully influences your subconscious mind.

Consider this: When you recall an experience, you don't just *see* it in your mind; you *feel* the emotions; you might remember the smells, sounds, or even the tactile sensations associated with that memory. The same principle applies when visualizing your desires.

For example, don't simply imagine the job title if your goal is to manifest a new career opportunity. Visualize yourself walking into the office or work environment, greeting your colleagues, and feeling confident and fulfilled. Hear the sounds of your workspace, smell the aroma of fresh coffee, or even feel the texture of the materials in your environment. In doing so, you engage all aspects of your subconscious mind, accelerating the manifestation process.

Trusting the Creative Process

Now, you might ask: *How can I reverse this habitual process of perceiving the world and create my own reality?* The answer is simple yet profound: you already use natural processes to your advantage in many areas of life. Just as you can steer a car in the direction you want, you can also direct your thought processes toward a desired outcome rather than being a victim of what your senses tell you.

Consider a familiar example: Imagine you are dealing with financial difficulties. When faced with such a situation, most people accept it as their "reality" and react accordingly.

They feel stressed, anxious, or hopeless, reinforcing the adverse conditions that created the problem in the first place. But there is an alternative.

Rather than accepting this as your permanent reality, you can use your mind to envision a new financial future. Start by forming a mental image of abundance. Picture yourself living without financial strain. Visualize money flowing easily into your life. Feel the joy, relief, and security that accompany this abundance. By holding this image in your mind and trusting the process, you instruct your subconscious to create these conditions in your reality.

Clarity is essential. Many people fail to manifest a new reality because they are unclear about what they want. They have vague desires or conflicting thoughts that send mixed messages to their subconscious. To create the circumstances you desire, you must precisely define your goals. Only then can your conscious mind effectively impress these desires upon your subconscious.

The Power of Clear Intentions

When you have a specific, clearly defined desire—whether it relates to health, wealth, relationships, or personal growth—it's time to bring that desire to the Universal Mind for manifestation. But how do you do this?

Imagination is the key. Albert Einstein famously said, "Imagination is more important than knowledge." In the realm of creation, this couldn't be truer. Your imagination forms a mental image once you have a clear and well-defined desire. Even if the image is initially incomplete, your creative mind can refine and perfect it.

Visualize your desire as if it has already been fulfilled. Don't place your desire in the future—see it as your current reality. Imagine yourself living in this desired state and experiencing all the positive emotions that come with it. This emotional connection is crucial because the subconscious responds to feelings, not words or images.

As you visualize, hold that image in your mind for as long as possible. Make it vivid, real, and multisensory. The more lifelike your mental image, the faster your subconscious mind will move toward making it a reality.

For example, if you desire improved health, don't simply imagine yourself as "not sick." Instead, see yourself as already vibrant, full of energy, moving effortlessly, and living life with vitality. Feel the strength and well-being coursing through your body. Let your subconscious mind soak in these feelings and this image of radiant health, and it will begin to manifest those conditions in your life.

Emotional Energy: The Fuel for Manifestation

It's not just the image you create that matters but the emotional energy you attach to it. Emotions are the fuel that drives the manifestation process. The more emotion you pour into your visualization, the more your subconscious will respond powerfully.

For instance, don't just intellectually acknowledge the concept when you visualize abundance. **Feel** the joy, the relief, the excitement of financial freedom. How would your life change if you already had what you wanted? How would you feel in your body? What emotions would flood your mind? The more you can amplify these emotions, the stronger the impact on your subconscious mind.

Emotion is the language of the subconscious. It understands the intensity and vibrancy of feelings, which is why past emotional experiences are often so deeply ingrained in us. When you attach powerful emotions to your desires, you speak directly to your subconscious in a way that words or passive thoughts alone cannot accomplish.

Letting Go and Trusting the Universe

Once you have created a clear mental image of your desire and infused it with powerful emotions, you must learn the art of *letting go*. Many people struggle with this. They become so attached to their desire that they try to force its manifestation through sheer willpower, which can impede the process.

The creative process requires a delicate balance between focused intention and detached trust. Once you've impressed your desire onto your subconscious, release it. Trust that the Universal Mind, through your subconscious, is now orchestrating the conditions necessary to bring your desire into reality.

The conscious mind's job is to decide what you want and form a vivid image of it. But the subconscious mind does the heavy lifting. It knows how to align people, events, and circumstances in ways that your conscious mind could never predict. The more you trust in this process, the faster and more effortlessly your desires will manifest.

When you ask for something, ask with faith and certainty—not pleading or hoping. Your desire is already yours. When you plant the image in your subconscious mind, you've activated the forces that will bring it into your experience. This is why **faith** is so essential. It would be best to believe that what you desire is possible and inevitable. And that It's already on its way to you.

Aligning with Universal Laws

As you've realized, the subconscious mind has direct access to the Universal Mind—a vast and infinite intelligence that operates according to unchanging laws. These laws govern everything in the universe, from the rotation of the planets to the ebb and flow of your life circumstances. Once your subconscious mind accepts your desires, it taps into the Universal Mind to orchestrate everything needed to manifest your goals.

Your role is not micromanaging the process or dictating how things unfold. This is where many people go wrong—they believe they must control every detail of the manifestation process. However, just like you don't consciously regulate the complex processes in your body (such as your heartbeat or digestion), you don't need to control how your desire materializes.

Let go and trust the laws of the universe. Once your desire impresses the subconscious mind, the Universal Mind will arrange events, circumstances, and even people in your favor. What's important to understand here is that the Universal Mind operates in ways far beyond your conscious comprehension. It knows no limitations—it works with infinite resources and possibilities that extend well beyond your current awareness.

Here's a key point: **the timing of manifestation is in the hands of the Universal Mind**. You may not always see immediate results, but that doesn't mean your desire isn't coming. Impatience or doubt can disrupt the process, like digging up a seed too early can prevent it from sprouting. Keep in mind that the universe is constantly moving at perfect timing. Trust that things are unfolding at the right pace, even when nothing appears to be happening.

Faith and Patience: The Twin Pillars of Manifestation

Manifestation requires two qualities that often challenge our modern, fast-paced lifestyles: **faith and patience**.

Faith is the unwavering belief that your desire is already coming to you. It knows that the moment you impress an image onto your subconscious, the Universal Mind sets into motion everything needed to bring it into physical reality. Faith is about seeing with your inner eye, even when there is no external evidence yet. It's about maintaining a calm certainty that what you seek is already yours, even if it hasn't appeared in your life yet.

On the other hand, patience is about allowing the process to unfold in its own time. Just like planting a seed, you must trust that the manifestation will grow and bloom at the right moment. Rushing or doubting the process only interferes with its natural progression. True patience is an act of surrender—releasing control and trusting that the universe is doing its part.

Remember, **faith and patience work hand-in-hand**. Faith keeps your vision alive, while patience allows it to grow. Without faith, you may give up on your dreams prematurely. Without patience, you may try to force or manipulate the process, leading to frustration. Together, they form a powerful foundation for conscious creation.

The Tools of the Subconscious Mind

Once your subconscious mind has accepted the command of your desire, it immediately begins working through the vast resources of the Universal Mind. It draws on infinite possibilities, orchestrating people, events, and circumstances to fulfill your request. These resources are often unseen and operate in ways that transcend logical understanding.

Consider how often things you've desired or worried about seem to unfold in unexpected ways. This is no accident. The subconscious mind uses every tool at its disposal, from synchronicities to intuitive nudges, to bring about the conditions necessary for your manifestation.

Synchronicities, for instance, are seemingly coincidental events that align perfectly with your desires. Have you ever thought about someone, only to have them call you shortly afterward?

Or stumbled upon a piece of information right when you needed it? These aren't random occurrences—they are the results of your subconscious mind working with the Universal Mind to bring your desires into your life.

It's essential to stay open and attentive to these signs. **Synchronicities are like breadcrumbs**, leading you toward the fulfillment of your desire.

Follow them without question, even when they seem illogical or unexpected. The universe often communicates through subtle clues; recognizing them is part of the creative process.

Living in Harmony with Universal Laws

Once you understand the connection between your conscious, subconscious, and the Universal Mind, you begin to live in harmony with the universal laws that govern all creation. These laws are immutable—they don't change based on circumstance, opinion, or belief. They simply are.

One of the most important laws to remember is the **Law of Cause and Effect**. Every thought you think is a cause, and every result in your life is an effect. When you consciously choose your thoughts, you direct the causes that create the impact in your life. This law reminds us that nothing in life happens by accident or coincidence. Your reality directly reflects the causes you have set in motion through your thoughts and emotions.

Another fundamental law is the **Law of Vibration**, which states that everything in the universe, including your thoughts, is energy vibrating at a specific frequency. When you align your thoughts with the frequency of your desires—meaning you think, feel, and act as if your desires are already fulfilled—you naturally attract that same frequency into your life. This is why cultivating the emotional energy of gratitude, love, and joy is so powerful. These high-vibration states align you with the frequency of your desires, making manifestation effortless.

By understanding and working in harmony with these laws, you become a conscious creator of your reality. No longer a passive observer, you step into your rightful role as a co-creator with the universe.

Moving Forward: The Path to Mastery

To summarize the key concepts:

- **All creation begins in the imagination.** The thoughts and images you create in your mind shape the reality you experience.

- **Emotion is the driving force behind manifestation**. The subconscious mind responds to the intensity of your emotions. Feel your desires as though they are already confirmed.

- **Let go of the need to control the outcome.** Once you've impressed your desire on your subconscious, trust that the Universal Mind is working on your behalf. Release attachment to when or how your desire will manifest.

- **Faith and patience are essential**. Trust the process. Know that what you seek is already on its way, and allow the universe's timing to unfold without interference.

- **Synchronicities are signs**. Pay attention to the subtle clues and opportunities the universe places in your path. They are leading you toward your desired outcome.

- **Live in alignment with universal laws**. Understand that the Law of Cause and Effect and the Law of Vibration are constantly at work. Align your thoughts, feelings, and actions with the outcomes you wish to create, and the universe will respond in kind.

As you continue this journey, recognize that **you are always creating, consciously or unconsciously**. Your thoughts, emotions, and beliefs constantly shape your reality experience. The more you master the connection between your conscious and subconscious minds, the more powerfully you can direct the course of your life.

With this understanding, you are equipped to shape your reality consciously in alignment with your deepest desires. This is the essence of true Transformation—the realization that your life is not a series of random events but a deliberate creation of your thoughts and beliefs.

Are you ready to step fully into your power as a creator? As you continue on this path, the miraculous power of the universe will reveal itself to you. **The only limit is the limit you place on your imagination.**

Let us continue this journey together—toward a life where you consciously create the reality you wish to experience.

To You, The One on the Transformation Journey

By now, you've traveled through the first half of **TRANSFORMATION**, and I hope it's already begun to stir something meaningful within you. Whether these ideas have challenged your perspective, ignited new possibilities, or given you practical tools to start creating the life you envision, I want to thank you for the energy and time you've committed to this journey.

This process isn't just about reading—it's about experiencing a shift, an evolution, and I'm truly grateful that you've trusted these words to guide you. **Now, I'd love to hear about your transformation so far**. How has this journey felt to you? Have certain concepts resonated deeply or sparked new ways of thinking? Perhaps a chapter or idea has opened your mind or left you eager for more clarity or depth. Whatever your experience, your insights are invaluable to me.

Your perspective is unique, and your thoughts can help shape the remainder of this journey for yourself and those who will follow. **Transformation is a conversation between your inner self and the words you take in—and I believe your voice matters in this dialogue.**

So, if you feel inspired, I would love to hear what's resonating with you. What ideas or exercises have connected with you the most? Is there anything you feel could be expanded or deepened? Your feedback will help guide the path ahead, and together, we can ensure this journey continues to unfold in ways that serve your growth.

Thank you for embracing this transformation and for sharing your reflections. I look forward to hearing from you and continuing this powerful process together.

With deep gratitude and respect,

Choyo Gomex

CHAPTER V

The Key to Reprogramming Your Reality

By now, I'm going to assume you've chosen a **specific desire**—something you feel is missing from your life that would enhance your happiness. You've taken the time to shape this desire in your imagination, forming it into a **definitive thought-form**. That's an excellent start. But how do you take that mental image and impress it onto your **subjective mind,** where the real magic happens?

The key lies in how you "speak" to your subjective mind. And yes, you must communicate with it as if it were a distinct individual. Some people find directing this conversation toward their solar plexus helpful, as this is a vital link between the physical body and the **Universal Mind**. The solar plexus is often called the "abdominal brain" because it governs activities without conscious thought—like your heart beating or your digestion working without any effort.

Speaking to Your Subconscious Mind

When communicating with your **subjective mind**, you can speak mentally, especially when speaking aloud isn't convenient. But if possible, and when you're alone, it's powerful to say the words **out loud**. This verbalization helps crystallize the thought form and imprints it more deeply into your subconscious.

As we've discussed, **all answers are found in silence**, so practicing meditation is crucial. It would be best to have a calm sanctuary where you can be alone with your thoughts and concentrate on creating vivid images in your mind. Close your eyes, enter a state of peace, and try to feel the subtle energy of the **Universal Mind** flowing through your body, even if you don't physically sense it at first. At the very least, allow yourself to mentally accept this unseen force is an indisputable truth.

In this relaxed state, **bring the image of your desire to mind**. Picture it as clearly as you can and begin conversing with your subjective mind like a young child. Simple, direct, and full of conviction.

For example, you might say: "It is my desire and my will that you act on this project of mine. It is for my benefit and the benefit of all others involved." "I desire to be in perfect harmony with all creative activity."

"I know that through your connection to the Universal Mind, you have the power to accomplish this task, and I thank you for already making it a reality."

One essential thing to remember here is **gratitude**. Express gratitude as **if your desire has already been granted**, just as Jesus did in the Bible when He said, "I thank you, Father, because you hear me." Gratitude affirms that your request is worthy of being fulfilled, opening you to receive the manifestation more quickly.

The Law of Attraction at Work

Your **Subconscious Mind**, a function of the **Universal Mind**, impregnates the image you create with **energy and intent**. Through the **Law of Attraction**, the necessary elements for manifesting your desire begin to come together. Think of it this way: the mental image you've formed acts as a blueprint, and the **Universal Mind** must construct the corresponding circumstances in the physical world.

Let's use a metaphor to explain this: Imagine you have a cup filled with sulfuric acid. No matter where you dip a piece of wood into the acid, it will burn. The **acid's power** is present throughout the liquid. Similarly, the **Universal Mind** is present in all things at all times. Wherever your **thought touches** the Universal Mind, its full power is present. You only need to make **contact** at one point, and the **whole** is engaged in the process.

Letting Go of Control

One critical point to remember when conversing with your subjective mind is this: **Don't tell it how to do its job**. Through its connection to the Universal Mind, your subjective mind knows far more than you consciously do. Your role is not to micromanage the details but to trust that your subjective mind will orchestrate everything necessary for your desire's manifestation. Make your request simple, clear, and specific, but **leave the "how" up to your subconscious.** The details—timing, the people involved, or the circumstances—will fall into place in ways you could never have predicted.

In this process, the most important thing you need is **absolute faith**. This is not about so-called "faith healing" or miracles—this is a scientifically grounded practice. However, faith still plays a crucial role because it determines your **mental attitude** toward the process.

If you ask a friend to do something for you and immediately doubt whether they can handle it, how likely will they deliver their best effort? Similarly, if you communicate doubt to your subconscious, you undermine its ability to manifest your desires. The **Universal Mind** knows precisely how you feel because you are an **individual** of that mind. Therefore, you must trust its power, no matter how large or small your desire may be.

Scientific Proof of Imprinting Thoughts

If you're wondering whether it's possible to impress your thoughts on the **Universal Mind**, rest assured that **scientific studies** have demonstrated the ability to transfer thoughts from one mind to another. However, we are dealing with something far more powerful here—the **Universal Mind**, which contains the accumulated thoughts of **all individuals** across all time.

The **simplicity of this technique** is one of its greatest strengths. It's not complex, and the results you experience will depend largely on your mental attitude and your **spiritual faith**. Don't focus too much on the results themselves—those will come in their own time. Instead, work on cultivating a **positive, open attitude** and trust that the Universal Mind will respond.

A Practical Example

To illustrate how this works in real life, let me share a true story that perfectly embodies these principles. A man wanted to sell his house during a deep depression. The chances of selling his house were slim, and the statistics were grim. Houses weren't selling, and he knew it wouldn't be easy.

What did this man do? First, he acted in the **physical world**, just as anyone would. He placed his house with three different real estate agents, hoping that one of them might find a buyer. But he didn't stop there. He also acted on the **mental plane**, where the real power lies.

Every day, he created a vivid **mental image** of his house already sold. He didn't get bogged down in the details of how it would happen. He didn't imagine a specific buyer or speculate about the price. Instead, he focused on the **result**: his house sold, his bags packed, the movers arriving, and him driving away. He didn't just abstractly think about these things; he **visualized them in real-time**—as if they were happening in that moment. He saw the moving truck pull up, the boxes being packed, and himself saying goodbye to his home for the last time.

His objective mind worked to make the house available for sale, but he left the heavy lifting to his **subjective mind**. That same month, dozens of homes were put up for sale in his neighborhood. Only two of them sold, and his house was one of them. His thought form manifested precisely as he had visualized it—right down to waving goodbye as he drove away.

Using the Full Power of Your Mind

Sadly, 99% of people never use this knowledge. Most go through life wielding their **objective mind** like a plastic hammer, unaware that they have access to a **powerful sledgehammer** that can transform their reality. They rely on a weak, confused approach instead of leveraging the **limitless resources** of the **Universal Mind**.

Why do so many remain in the dark? It's because they don't understand the **laws of the Universe**. These laws are simple, clear, and unchanging: "Ask, and it will be given to you. Seek, and you will find. Knock, and the door will be opened to you."

Now, you know how to **ask**, how to **seek**, and how to **knock**. The principles are straightforward, and the methods are practical. But here's the thing: **knowing** what to do isn't enough. Your life will change not because you know **how** to manifest your desires but because you **do it.**

I've given you the tools. The rest is up to you. Only you can apply these techniques and set your subjective mind to work. **No one else can do this for you.** It would be best to take responsibility for your life and desires. The Universal Mind is ready and waiting to help you—it always has been. But it can only respond to the **commands you give it**.

The Power Is in Your Hands

Now that you understand how to impress your desires on the **Universal Mind**, it's time to take action. Start with something specific—something you truly want in your life. Use your imagination, create a vivid image, and impress it onto your **subjective mind**.

Then, **let go**, trust the process, and know that your desire is already on its way to manifest in your physical reality. The more you practice this, the more your life will transform.

The **law of the Universe** is on your side, and the only limit to what you can achieve is the limit you impose on yourself.

Let's Make It More Practical

To ensure this process is as practical as possible, let's walk through it step-by-step once more:

1. **Clarify Your Desire:** Be specific. What exactly do you want? Is it a financial goal, a relationship, a new career, or improved health? Get crystal clear on what you want and

why you want it. This clarity helps you form a distinct **thought-form.**

2. **Create a Mental Image**: Now that you know what you want, **visualize** it in as much detail as possible. Don't see it as something that will happen in the future—see it as **already happening**. What does it look like? What does it feel like? Smell like? Hear like? Use your five senses to bring the image to life.

3. **Impress the Image on Your Subconscious**: In a quiet place, enter a relaxed state through meditation or deep breathing. With your mind calm and focused, bring the image to the forefront. Then, **speak to your subconscious mind**. Tell it, with conviction, what you desire and that it is already happening. Use phrases like, "This is already mine," "I am so grateful for this," and "Thank you for manifesting this."

4. **Let Go and Trust the Process**: After impressing your desire on your subconscious, **release it**. Don't obsess over how or when it will happen. Trust that the **Universal Mind** is working on your behalf, and everything necessary to manifest your desire is already in motion. The details will take care of themselves.

5. **Practice Gratitude**: Maintain an attitude of gratitude as if you've already received your desire. Gratitude keeps you in harmony with the creative power of the **Universal Mind** and reinforces your belief in the process.

6. **Faith in Action: Faith isn't just passive**. While trusting the process, you must also stay open to **opportunities** that arise. These opportunities may be the very means by which your subconscious mind brings your desire to fruition. Act when prompted, but don't try to force the outcome.

Why Gratitude Is Essential

Gratitude plays a crucial role in this process. When you express gratitude for something you haven't yet physically received, you are telling the **Universal Mind** that you believe in the reality of your desire. You are affirming that it already exists in the **mental plane** and will soon manifest in the **physical plane**.

Gratitude acts as a **magnet**, drawing what you desire toward you. It aligns you with the frequency of abundance, prosperity, and fulfillment. The more grateful you are, the more you will attract situations and circumstances that match this energy.

As mentioned earlier, Jesus continually expressed thanks before his miracles took place. He gave thanks in advance, knowing that the manifestation of his desires was inevitable. You can do the same.

Cultivating Absolute Faith

Faith is not wishful thinking—it's a knowing, a deep conviction that the **Universal Mind** can and will respond to your commands. Faith is strengthened through experience. The more you practice this process and see results, the stronger your faith becomes.

It's also important to understand that faith is not just about believing that the **Universal Mind** will respond but about believing in **your worthiness**. You must have faith that you are deserving of the things you desire. Often, people fail to manifest their dreams because they secretly believe they are unworthy. Your **subconscious mind** picks up on this doubt, which can block the manifestation process.

You must have absolute **confidence** that you are worthy of your desires and have the power to bring them into reality. Once you align with this truth, the Universe will respond to your every command.

Another Example of Success

Let's look at another example. A woman deeply desired a career change but faced constant rejection in her job search. She knew she needed more than just sending out resumes—she needed to

reprogram her reality. She used the process outlined in this chapter, creating a vivid image of herself already in the new role. She saw herself in the office, wearing the new clothes she would wear to work, interacting with her new colleagues, and feeling fulfilled by the job. Every detail was evident in her mind. She spoke to her **subconscious mind** as if she were already working in that position, affirming that the job was hers and thanking the Universe for making it a reality. She kept this image alive and let it settle into her subconscious.

Within weeks, a company contacted her about a job she hadn't even applied for. The position was exactly what she had visualized, down to the smallest details. The job offer came quickly, and she began working in her envisioned career.

The Final Word: You Have the Power

The truth is, you already have the power to reprogram your reality—you always have. You are an **individual expression** of the **Universal Mind**, and with this connection, there is nothing you cannot achieve, manifest, or experience. All it takes is learning how to **communicate** with your subconscious, forming clear, vivid mental images, and having **faith** that the process will work.

Remember, **every great achievement** begins in the imagination. Whether you want to transform your health, finances, relationships, or personal growth, it all starts with a **thought form**. Once that thought form is impressed upon the **subconscious**, the Universal Mind will take over, organizing the elements necessary to bring it into reality.

But the power lies in your hands. As I've emphasized before, knowing what to do is not enough. You must **apply** this knowledge consistently and with conviction. Consistent practice will only develop the faith and mastery necessary to reprogram your life in alignment with your deepest desires. So, what will you create next? What area of your life are you ready to transform? The potential is limitless, and now, so is your understanding. With this knowledge, you can shape the reality you choose.

The tools are in your hands. The rest is up to you.

Start today. Don't wait. There's no better time than now to begin **reprogramming your reality.**

CHAPTER VI

The Art of Creating Your Future

Before we delve further into this study, let's take a closer look at how your **thought form** operates. When properly imprinted onto the **Universal Mind**, it will eventually materialize into tangible objects, events, or circumstances in your life. We've touched on this concept already, but it's worth a deeper dive to truly grasp the significance of the **Law of Attraction**, which governs how your thought forms interact with the universe.

We've all heard the phrase "opposites attract" and "likes repel." While this is a well-known physical law, especially in electricity and magnetism, we often overlook how it applies to the broader workings of the universe, particularly in mental and spiritual realms. But if we observe closely, we'll notice this law operates across all aspects of nature and existence.

Now, let's focus on how you can **harness this law** to bring your **legitimate desires** into your life by intentionally creating thought forms. The **universal substance**—the fabric of existence—manifests the two polarities of **matter and spirit**. These polarities naturally seek expression in the material world. In their quest for balance and harmony, the forces of nature generate tremendous activity, which leads to all action and reaction, life and growth. This principle is at the heart of how **thought forms** become reality.

The Journey from Thought to Reality

Your thought form is birthed in the **invisible, inner world** of your mind. This is the positive polarity. From there, it seeks its **negative polarity**—its material counterpart—in the physical world. In other words, your **thought** is the seed, and the **material manifestation** of that thought is the sprouting plant.

Everything you see around you—the objects in your environment, relationships, career, and health—are the **visible results of invisible thought forms**. Just as nature operates with precision when turning a seed into a tree, so too does the **Universal Mind** when transforming your thought forms into tangible outcomes.

But how long does it take for a thought form to manifest? This depends on many factors. The complexity of your thought form, the involvement of other people, and the **obstacles** you need to overcome all influence the timing. Just as some plants grow quickly and others take years to mature fully, your thought form will **manifest in its own time**, according to its nature.

Thought Forms and the Law of Attraction

The **Law of Attraction** plays a pivotal role in how thought forms materialize. This law—deeply rooted in **metaphysics, psychology**, and **mental science**—dictates that like attracts like. The thoughts you dwell on, the images you hold in your mind, and the emotions you attach to these images all work together to **attract** similar energy from the universe.

To understand this process, think of your thought form like a seed planted in fertile soil. The seed contains everything necessary to grow into a full-fledged plant, but it needs the **right conditions** to flourish. Just as you wouldn't plant a seed in rocky soil and expect a healthy plant, you shouldn't attempt to manifest your desires if your mental environment is cluttered with doubt, fear, or limiting beliefs.

Before planting your thought form, you must **clear the ground**. This means removing the **mental weeds**—the stones of envy, the debris of laziness, and the limiting beliefs that hinder your growth. Once the mental soil is prepared, you can plant your thought form with **intention** and care, imprinting it onto the **Universal Mind**. This is much like planting a seed in rich, fertile soil.

After planting, you must nurture your thought form just as you would water and nourish a seed. This doesn't mean **obsessing** over it or constantly checking to see if it's growing. Instead, it requires **faith**—a belief that the **invisible powers of the Universe** are at work, even if you can't see immediate results.

The Power of Patience and Persistence

One of the most challenging parts of the manifestation process is the waiting period between planting the **thought-form** and seeing its physical manifestation. Just as a seed takes time to sprout, your thought forms will take time to **germinate and grow**. The timeline depends on factors like complexity, the number of people involved, and the obstacles to overcome.

But here's the beauty of it: once you've planted your thought form in the **Universal Mind**, it will **inevitably sprout**—as long as you remain patient and persistent. Just as roots spread from a growing plant, lines of force will radiate from your thought form, gathering the necessary elements for its physical expression.

There will come a day when the first small sprout of your thought form appears in your reality. It might be a subtle change—an unexpected opportunity, a new contact, or a shift in circumstances. This first sign is an **important milestone** because it signals that the **manifestation process** is working. From there, your role is to continue nurturing the thought form with meditation, **positive expectation, and gratitude**.

The Seed of Thought: A Miraculous Process

To further illustrate this process, let's consider the analogy of planting a **seed**. Before planting, carefully choose a seed that will produce the desired plant or flower. You wouldn't plant a seed randomly or without care—this same principle applies to your **thought forms**. The seed represents your thought form, and you must choose it carefully based on your **desire**.

Once planted, you don't disturb the seed. You trust that nature's creative processes will bring it to life, even though you can't see them working. In the same way, once you've planted your thought form in the **Universal Mind**, you must **resist the urge to interfere** or worry about how it will manifest. Trust that the invisible powers of the universe are nurturing your thought form, just as nature nurtures the seed.

Your task is to **cooperate with the Universal Mind**, much like you would cooperate with nature by watering and providing sunlight for a seed. In this case, your cooperation involves creating a peaceful environment through **meditation** and maintaining faith in the **manifestation process**. The more you focus on your desire with certainty and expectation, the more quickly your thought form will grow into a physical reality.

Faith: The Key Ingredient

This entire process requires **faith**. Just as the first person to plant a seed needed faith to wait for the harvest, so too must you have faith in your thought forms. The power of faith is often misunderstood, but it's the essential element that ensures the **transformation from thought to reality**.

Without faith, you'll be tempted to dig up your thought form before it has a chance to grow, doubting whether it will ever manifest. But if you persist, believing your thought form is taking root and growing, you will eventually see the results.

Faith allows you to believe in something that **hasn't yet manifested** in the material world. It's the confidence that your thought form exists in the **spiritual realm** and is simply awaiting the right time to become visible. This is why the Master said, "Whatever you ask for in prayer, believe that you have received it, and it will be yours." It would be best to believe you already have what you've asked for, even when your senses tell you otherwise.

The Role of Belief in Success

This concept of **believing before seeing** may initially seem counterintuitive, but it is the key to successful manifestation. The degree to which you can bring your mind to **accept this truth** will determine whether or not your thought forms manifest. It's not enough to wish for something—you must believe it is already yours.

To illustrate this, let's consider an example from everyday life. When you take a photo with your phone, that **image** is immediately stored in a digital space—perhaps in the cloud. The landscape in the photo may change over time, but the image remains fixed, accessible at any time from anywhere. Similarly, when you imprint your thought form in the **Universal Mind**, it remains in that intangible space, ready to manifest when the conditions are right.

Your thought form is **indestructible** because the **Universal Mind** is eternal and immortal. Once imprinted, your thought form exists permanently, and it will **inevitably manifest** in the material world, just as long as you remain aligned with its realization.

The Indispensable Role of Belief

One of the biggest challenges is believing your desire has already been fulfilled when your physical senses tell you otherwise. This is where true **spiritual maturity** comes in. It's not about ignoring reality but understanding that the **spiritual** precedes the **physical**. Every material object, circumstance, or situation begins as a thought form. Believing in this process is essential.

When you plant the seed in your mind, the Universal Mind begins working to bring it to fruition. But it would be best if you held on to your belief, even when there are no visible signs of progress. Only through this sustained belief will you see your thought forms take root, grow, and eventually bloom into reality.

Conclusion: The Art of Creating Your Future

In this chapter, we've explored the intricate process of how **thought forms** work and how they manifest through the **Law of Attraction**. You now understand that just as a seed grows into a plant, so does a **thought form** manifest into your reality.

But the most important lesson to take away is this: **faith and patience** are the keys.

Once you've planted the seed of your desire in the **Universal Mind**, you must trust the process and **believe** it is already working in your favor, even if you can't yet see the results. Like a farmer who plants a seed and waits patiently for it to grow, you must maintain

faith and **persistence**, knowing that your thought form is developing below the surface.

Remember, everything in your external world began as an idea, a mental image, a thought form. You are constantly planting these seeds in your mind, consciously or unconsciously. Creating your future involves **consciously choosing** the seeds you want to grow and **nurturing them** with focused attention and belief.

The results may not always come as quickly as you'd like, but they will come. And when they do, you'll look back and understand the power of the process you've been cultivating. The **Law of Attraction** is as natural and dependable as the laws of physics—it's always in operation, whether you believe in it or not. The choice is yours: will you use this knowledge to create your desired future, or will you let random, unconscious thought forms continue to shape your reality?

Act Now

As you move forward, begin **consciously applying** the principles you've learned in this chapter. Here's a quick recap of the steps to creating your future:

1. **Clarify your desire:** Know precisely what you want. Be specific and ensure it aligns with your highest values and goals.
2. **Create a thought form:** Visualize your desire in vivid detail. See it, feel it, experience it as if it has already happened.
3. **Imprint it on the Universal Mind:** Enter a meditative state and impress this image onto your subconscious. Speak to your **subjective mind** with clarity, confidence, and gratitude.
4. **Release it:** Let go of attachment to the outcome and trust that the Universal Mind will take care of the "how."
5. **Maintain faith and patience:** Keep your belief strong. Avoid doubting the process and stay committed to nurturing your desire with positive expectations.

6. **Take inspired action:** When opportunities arise, act. The **Universal Mind** often works through channels you least expect, so stay open to possibilities.

Now that you understand the **art of creating your future**, you have the tools to shape your life in any direction you choose. You are a powerful creator; the universe is your partner in this journey. **Your thoughts, desires, and beliefs are the seeds** of your reality. What will you plant today?

The future is yours to create. Don't wait for circumstances to change—**change your thoughts**, and you will change your life. By mastering the art of creating your future, you can unlock a life of **abundance**, joy, and **fulfillment.**

Please take a moment now to reflect on what you truly want in life and then begin the process of bringing it into existence. The Universal Mind is listening, waiting for your command. **What will you create next?**

Final Thought: The Future Is Yours to Shape

In closing, remember that your **future is not predetermined**. It is shaped by the thoughts you think, the images you hold, and the beliefs you embrace. Every moment is an opportunity to plant new seeds, to create new thought forms, and to direct your life toward the fulfillment of your greatest dreams. The art of creating your future is a lifelong practice, one that becomes easier and more powerful with time and experience.

You are the **architect of your destiny**. With each passing day, you are given a fresh canvas on which to paint the reality you desire. So, go forward with confidence, knowing that you have the power to **create your future**—a future that reflects your highest aspirations, your deepest desires, and the **limitless potential** that resides within you.

The time to start is now. **Your future awaits**—and now it's yours to create.

CHAPTER VII

The Cycle of Giving and Receiving

When you begin studying thought forms and integrating them into your mental toolkit, you embark on one of the most profound journeys of your life: the conscious creation of your reality. This shift represents not just a change in thinking but a complete transformation in how you engage with the world. You are no longer a passive observer but an active architect of your circumstances.

Consciously shaping your reality isn't something most people even consider, let alone attempt. We often drift through life, reacting to circumstances and believing that fate or external forces hold the cards. But the moment you decide to take control—when you realize that your thoughts, beliefs, and intentions can mold your external environment—you have taken your first steps into the kindergarten of conscious creation.

Of course, these first steps can be awkward, much like a toddler learning to walk. At first, you may stumble, fall, and experience frustration. But through persistence and faith, you eventually stand firm, taking those initial steps with growing confidence. It's a transformative moment that opens up a world of unlimited possibilities. There is joy in this newfound ability, unlike anything else in life. You have tapped into a source of power that few people even know exists, and with it, you can reshape your entire reality.

This awakening to the power of thought forms often feels like an awakening to a deeper spiritual truth. When you fully grasp the idea that everything you need to overcome life's obstacles is already within you, an exhilarating realization takes hold: you are not limited by the world around you but are empowered to shape it. The seed of your success lies within your consciousness, ready to grow as soon as you recognize its existence.

At this point, you may think that this all sounds exaggerated or impossible. That's understandable if you haven't yet experienced the power of conscious creation. But as someone reading these words, you are already on the path to understanding these more profound mysteries. Your curiosity alone is evidence of your spiritual and mental advancement. This knowledge is not random—it comes to those who are ready for it, to those who have earned the right to explore the powers of the mind.

A Universal Law: The Principle of Thought Forms

Nature, as wise as it is, wastes nothing. This knowledge would have remained hidden if you were not ready to wield this power. However, you can use it now that you have stumbled upon it. But be warned—this is not a power to be used lightly. The principle of giving and receiving is inextricably linked to how you wield this creative force. Any thought form you create will return to you, carrying the energy and intention with which it was imbued.

"Many are called, but few are chosen" is an ancient phrase that can be applied here. Perhaps, more accurately, we could say: "Many are told, but few choose to listen."

You have the choice of whether to embrace or ignore this power. If you use it for selfish or harmful purposes, you will surely regret it. Though intangible, every action has consequences, and thoughts are no exception to this universal law.

Thought forms are, quite literally, the bread you cast upon the waters, returning to you multiplied. Your thoughts are the bread, and the waters represent the vast, infinite ocean of the subconscious mind. When you impress an idea onto the subconscious, it doesn't merely sit idle; it works tirelessly to transform that idea into a reality in the material world.

This is why cleaning yourself of negative emotions like jealousy, resentment, and bitterness is critical before using thought forms. Think of it as trying to build a house on a lot full of debris. If the foundation isn't clean and clear, anything you try to build will eventually collapse. The universe, or the infinite mind, responds to purity of intention. If your heart is clouded with negative feelings, the thought forms you create will be equally clouded, and their outcomes will reflect that.

Cultivating Your Mental Garden

Before you start working with thought forms to create specific changes in your life, take some time to cleanse your mental and emotional space. Rid yourself of feelings that weigh you down or block your creative energies. This may take some time and effort, but it is a vital step in aligning yourself with the creative forces of the universe.

Once you've done this, you can begin to visualize yourself as a conduit of the Universal Mind. See yourself as an instrument receiving inspiration and guidance not only for your benefit but also for the benefit of others. Some people find it helpful to imagine themselves standing in the light of the Sun, receiving rays of divine power and illumination. This is a potent image because the Sun symbolizes life, warmth, and growth—qualities that are essential to the creative process.

Now, the thought forms you create should be uniquely yours. Don't rely on pre-packaged ideas or templates from others; these will not have the same impact. Instead, meditate on your intentions. Let the idea you wish to manifest mature in your mind, and only when you are completely satisfied with it should you begin to visualize it as already accomplished. Return to this mental image often, adding details and refining it as your vision grows clearer.

The more time you spend shaping and refining your thought forms, the more aligned they will be with your deeper desires and purpose. When you hold these visualizations long enough, they become a blueprint for your external reality. The key is consistency. Sporadic focus won't produce results, but steady, consistent mental energy will magnetize the results toward you. It's much like a garden—if you tend to it daily, it will bear fruit, but neglect leads to withering and decay.

Thought Forms in Action: Historical Examples

Many of the world's most successful people have tapped into this power, often without knowing it. While they may not have called it "thought forms," they intuitively grasped the principle that focused intention can shape reality. Consider the example of Elon Musk. He had a vision of sending ships into space, but the world's leading engineers told him it couldn't be done with the available technology. Instead of accepting defeat, Musk used his focused desire and imagination to create a solution. Today, he is one of the few entities—alongside entire nations—capable of sending rockets into space.

Napoleon, too, understood this principle, even if he didn't use the language of thought forms. When asked about obstacles, he famously replied, "I make circumstances." Napoleon understood that external circumstances were not immovable; the power of a clear and focused will could shape them.

Beethoven, despite being deaf, "heard" his symphonies within his mind, translating his inner vision into compositions that still resonate with audiences today. His burning desire to manifest his inner world into physical form allowed him to overcome his body's limitations. His thought forms were powerful enough to transcend even the limitations imposed by his physical senses.

Similarly, Thomas Edison once said, "I have not failed. I've just found 10,000 ways that won't work." Edison was a master at holding the thought form of success despite temporary setbacks. His tenacity and mental focus were crucial for manifesting his inventions, many of which revolutionized the world. Edison understood, consciously or not, that the power of holding a focused thought form could bend reality to his will.

Another compelling example of thought forms at work comes from the world of athletics. High-performing athletes often use a technique known as "visualization" to mentally rehearse their victories before they even compete. This practice involves creating a vivid mental image of success, from crossing the finish line to the crowd's cheers. It's no coincidence that many Olympic champions attribute their success to the power of visualization, essentially creating a powerful thought form. In these cases, the athletes' minds and bodies align with their visualized success, making it more likely to materialize in reality.

The Ripple Effect of Thought Forms

Now, you may wonder: How can my thoughts affect the world around me? How do these thought-forms ripple outward to shape circumstances beyond my immediate control? The answer lies in the interconnectedness of all things. Just as a single drop of water creates ripples across the surface of a pond, a single thought form sends energetic vibrations out into the universe, subtly influencing the events and people around you.

Imagine your mind as a tuning fork. When struck with the right intention, it vibrates at a frequency that aligns with the reality you wish to create. The law of attraction, another term frequently used in spiritual and self-help circles, functions similarly.

The vibration of your thought forms attracts experiences, people, and circumstances that resonate with your emitting frequency.

This is why it's so important to be deliberate with your thoughts. Negative, fear-based thoughts create a reality filled with obstacles, while positive, love-based thoughts open doors to new opportunities. The energy you put into the world always comes back to you in one form or another, so thought forms are often described as energy boomerangs.

Even scientific studies in quantum physics suggest that consciousness plays a role in shaping reality. The famous "observer effect" shows that mere observation can influence particles' behavior at the quantum level. This is strikingly similar to how thought forms work on a broader scale. When you focus on a particular outcome, your consciousness helps bring that outcome into being.

Practical Tips for Creating Thought Forms

So, how can you begin using thought forms to create positive changes in your life? The process starts with clarity. Define what you truly want and ensure that your intentions align with the highest good—for yourself and others. A thought-form grounded in selfish or harmful desires will backfire, but one created from a place of love, gratitude, and service will multiply and grow.

1.   **Clarity of Intention**: Before you even begin to visualize, spend some time reflecting on your desires. What do you truly want to manifest in your life? Is it aligned with your values and the greater good? Ensure that your intention is something you can fully believe in and commit to. Ambiguity in thought creates ambiguity in results.

2.   **Visualization**: Once your intention is clear, create a vivid mental image of the outcome you want to achieve. Imagine how it looks, feels, sounds, and smells in as much detail as possible. This isn't just daydreaming. It's about embedding the desired outcome deeply into your subconscious mind, where it can take root and begin to grow. Visualize yourself already in possession of this outcome. The subconscious doesn't differentiate between real and imagined, so mentally rehearsing your success, you're programming your mind to bring it into being.

3.   **Emotional Energy**: Thought forms are charged by emotion. The stronger and more positive the emotion you associate with your thought form, the more energy it will have to manifest. Feel the joy, relief, excitement, and gratitude of already having what you desire. This emotional energy acts like fuel, propelling your thought form into reality faster and with greater potency.

4.   **Faith and Expectation**: Once you've planted the seed of your thought form, nurturing it with faith is vital. Just as a farmer doesn't dig up their crops to see if they're growing, you must trust that your thought form is working behind the scenes. Faith creates a mental atmosphere of expectation, which attracts the desired result. Doubt and fear are like weeds that choke the growth of your thought form, so make sure to guard your mental garden.

5.   **Action**: Thought forms are not a substitute for action but a complement to it. When you create a thought form, be prepared to follow through with the actions necessary to bring it into reality. The universe will present you with opportunities, but you must take the steps required to manifest them physically. This can range from making a phone call, taking a class, or simply saying "yes" to the opportunities that arise.

6.   **Persistence**: Manifestation doesn't always happen overnight. Thought forms need time to grow and gather the necessary resources to materialize.

7.   The bigger the intention, the more time and energy it may require. Stay persistent, even when results aren't immediately visible. Remember that the universe works in its own time, but it will respond to your consistent mental energy.

Thought Forms and the Law of Reciprocity

One of the most powerful principles governing thought forms is the law of reciprocity—what you give out, you receive back. This cosmic truth operates on both material and energetic levels. Practically, your thoughts and actions create ripples that inevitably return to you.

The cycle of giving and receiving is a universal law. When you send out positive, generous, and loving thought forms, the universe will reflect these back to you in various ways. This could be in the form of unexpected opportunities, supportive relationships, or even tangible success. Conversely, if your thought forms are rooted in fear, resentment, or selfishness, you will attract those same qualities into your life.

Thought Forms in Relationships

The power of thought forms extends beyond your personal ambitions and can profoundly affect your relationships. Every thought you think about someone else sends energy in their direction. Your relationship with them will deteriorate if you constantly harbor negative thoughts about a person. Conversely, loving, positive, and forgiving thoughts can heal even the most strained relationships.

Consider this: How often do you focus on the shortcomings of others, projecting judgmental or critical thought forms? Imagine instead shifting your focus to their strengths, potential, and positive qualities. This shift in your own thought forms will change the energy between you and that person, improving the relationship on both sides.

This principle applies not just to romantic or familial relationships but also to professional and social interactions. Successful people often intuitively understand this; they exude confidence, positivity, and vision, which attracts others to them like a magnet.

Expanding the Cycle: Creating Global Change

While much of the focus of thought forms is personal growth, the principles can be expanded to bring about collective or global change. If enough people focus on positive, constructive thought forms for the world—peace, abundance, environmental healing, and equality—the collective energy of those thought forms will start influencing the global consciousness.

This is the foundation of movements like collective prayer, global meditation events, and intention circles.

When groups of people come together with aligned thought forms, the ripple effect is magnified exponentially. Imagine the power we could unleash if large groups of people consistently visualized solutions to global issues such as poverty, conflict, or climate change. The potential for transformation on a planetary scale becomes a dream and a reachable reality.

You are not just a passive participant in life but an integral part of a greater whole. Your thought forms contribute to the collective consciousness, and through deliberate, conscious creation, you can be part of the solution to the world's challenges. This is the ultimate expression of the cycle of giving and receiving.

Conclusion: You Are the Creator of Your Reality

The power to shape your reality is within you. Through the conscious creation of thought forms, you can align yourself with the infinite creative forces of the universe and bring your desires into material reality. The question is not whether you can create but whether you will choose to use this power consciously and constructively.

The cycle is simple: give and receive. What you put into the world—thoughts, intentions, and actions—will return to you, often multiplied. The process is about manifesting your desires and becoming a more conscious, deliberate, and aligned participant in the ongoing creation of reality.

By cultivating thought forms based on love, generosity, and positivity, you align yourself with the natural flow of abundance in the universe. And as you give out those energies, they will inevitably return to you in ways that may exceed your expectations. This way, you can create your desired life and contribute to a more harmonious and prosperous world.

The choice is yours. Will you continue to drift along, shaped by external circumstances, or will you step into your power as a conscious creator of your destiny?

CHAPTER VIII

The Mirror of Your Life

Once again, I ask you to be patient and not skip over the technical details.

Solidifying a fundamental idea before moving on to the finer points is always best. The idea I suggest you focus on is this: act daily with complete faith that your basic thought form is working. This may not seem very important to you, but I can assure you that it is.

Listing a long series of "don'ts" when using thought forms would be easy. But instead, let's concentrate on one big DO for the moment. We'll find that, by inference, it will provide us with all the "don'ts."

Now (listen) read this carefully: the degree of success you will enjoy using thought-forms will correspond precisely to the degree to which your habitual attitude toward life is constructive. Why? Because your habitual attitude toward life reflects your underlying real thought-form. If it's constructive, your results will be as well. And vice versa.

As an example, consider what would happen if a single drop of white paint were mixed into a can of black paint. What would you get? Black paint.

Now, suppose a man's mind is filled with dark thoughts. And consider, by chance, he had a small white thought. Obviously, his mind would still be filled with dark thoughts, correct?

Going further, if a man poured a stream of dark thoughts into the Universe over several years and suddenly introduced a small white thought, the Universe would remain a black sea for him. Do you agree? These dark thoughts wouldn't necessarily be what we typically call "bad." They could be due to neglect, doubt, hesitation, unhappiness, or distrust. But this man can't expect that only one constructive thought form will immediately undo the damage of millions of destructive thought forms that he has unconsciously imprinted in the Universe. Such a man may require years of effort to undo his previous actions (thoughts) made (done) out of ignorance. These seem like very harsh statements, but we can be sure that the "evil" will disappear forever once this has been accomplished. Or, put another way, as we've heard somewhere: "Our sins are forgiven."

Now, consider the man of good heart, jovial, cheerful, and naturally optimistic. His primary life thought form is constructive, and it has been for years. For him, in contrast to the pessimist, the Universe is white, and even in his occasional moment of weakness, it won't noticeably darken. Thus, things will come easily for the optimistic man, but life will be a heavy burden for the pessimist. I'm sure you have realized this over time. And this is the compelling scientific reason you've observed for that fact: the optimistic man, with good hopes, often creates favorable conditions for himself through his inherent thought form, perhaps unconscious; nonetheless, it is effective. On the other hand, the pessimistic individual creates his own "bad" conditions through a similar process.

So, now we can see that what we call "good and bad" are exact manifestations of the same law, applied differently but triggered by the same power, without any discrimination. Only in the long run does the good prevail over the bad, or evolution will be inconceivable.

If you analyze the previous comments, you'll discover an apparent paradox. We told one man that the Universe is white, and then we told another man that it's black. But there can only be one Universe. How can it be both black and white at the same time? The answer is that the Universe itself doesn't change, but the individual's perception varies, from pure white to pure black—or from pure goodness to pure evil.

Am I saying that the Universe is different for different people? My dear friend, that's precisely what I'm saying.

Now, for the moment, let's put aside the term "universal" and use a word that means "universal." That word is: "God." Let's remain calm and consider this word on its own merits. So, God is different for people because each individual creates their conception of God.

A well-known critic expressed one of the most profound truths of religion. You've probably heard the saying: "An honest man is the noblest work of God." Robert Ingersoll, skillfully and cynically, inverted that saying, thus pointing out to mental scientists what is genuinely the entirety of their creed. He said: "An honest God is the noblest work of man."

Think about it again. If you've followed these discussions carefully, you should see that, in a certain sense, each person creates their own God. I say this with all due reverence because you understand that this means each person decides what God should be for them or if you prefer, what the Universal Mind will do for them.

Are you surprised to learn that theologians have fought for centuries over the definition of God? How could they have agreed, given that they differ in nature? However, we don't need to pause because of their disputes. All we need to know is that we have the almost miraculous power to create our conception of God.

Think about it carefully... We say He is, but do we act and speak daily as if we believe He is just? Then, He is just. We think He will provide us with all good things, but do we act daily as if we believe that? Then, He gives us all good things. We believe that He will respond to a constructive thought form by making it happen, and do we act daily as if we think that? Then, He will make it happen. It's that simple!

And that is the meaning in the scriptural warnings: "As a man thinks in his heart, so is he." Do you realize? It doesn't refer to what the man says but to what he thinks. And not what he thinks occasionally when he remembers to think about it. It's what he believes in his heart—daily, habitually, and without reservations. That's what he is in the world of thought, and that's precisely what he becomes in the objective world.

The mental scientist dedicated to his task will show the world an admirable set of personal virtues.

His actions will be spectacular and perhaps even seem foolish to some critical minds because he isn't continuously planning in his interest. But how fabulously superior is this mental scientist? That great lesson he has learned leads him to leave the means and resources to the "Universal Committee of Means and Resources" once he has decided the direction and manner in which that power will manifest in HIS life.

Attention: This doesn't mean he sits back comfortably and does nothing! Far from it! He will be decidedly active. He was performing his duties and doing things well.

And, as the greatest of the Masters told us: "Do not worry about tomorrow," the mental scientist strictly adheres to this rule and has well summarized this thought in an immortal stanza that would be his Psalm of life: "Trust no future, no matter how pleasant! Let the dead past bury its dead. Act, act in the living present. With the heart, and with God ahead."

The person who knows how to work with thought forms doesn't worry about whether or not they will get their reward. They KNOW they will receive it. They radiate joy and confidence, not because "someone else told them so," but because they simply can't act any other way. They know their existence has real meaning, and they are eager to record their positive experiences in the book of their life. They constantly seek opportunities to expand their sphere of influence, both with ideas and with people. They know that love and beauty go hand in hand with lifestyle as twin agents of the Universal Mind, and they find them equally in the joyful laughter of a child, in the piece of soft clay, in the dancing rays of the Sun, in the caress of a loved one, or in the smile of a friend. Being in tune with the Universal Mind and its infinite generosity, such a person lives in a world of wonders that far surpasses material wealth.

Can anyone honestly doubt that such a world exists and is within reach? This world is not a distant fantasy but a reality waiting to be unlocked. The key lies not in some external force but within your thoughts, intentions, and actions. You have always possessed this key, and now, more than ever, it is time to use it.

To enter this new world, you must shape your thoughts with intention. Every thought holds power. What you focus on consistently will shape your experience. This isn't just wishful thinking—it's a proven truth. History shows that those who succeed and live fully are those who understand the power of belief combined with action. Your thoughts are not passive reflections of the world; they are active forces that shape it.

The key to this world is simple: it's your thought patterns. What are you consistently thinking about? What occupies your mental space? These thoughts aren't just fleeting—they are creating your reality, moment by moment. This isn't just about positive thinking but about intentional thinking. It's about directing your mental energy toward the life you want to create.

Right now, in this very moment, you are closer than ever to unlocking this truth. You don't need another book, seminar, or a new idea. You already have everything you need to create the life you want. The essence of this idea is within you. The time for action is now.

Imagine standing at the door of the world you've always dreamed of. You hold the key, but it's up to you to turn it.

This requires belief—belief in yourself, in the process, and in the power of your thoughts. Although it may feel unfamiliar initially, that discomfort is simply a sign that you're stepping into a new way of being.

In this world, you'll no longer be a passive observer; from now on, you can be an active creator. See, your challenges not obstacles but opportunities to refine your focus and strengthen your will. The world is ready for you, but it requires your full participation. You must show up confident that your thoughts and actions are aligned with the reality you wish to manifest.

This is not a world for the doubter. It is for the one who is ready to claim their power. The door will not open for those who hesitate. However, if you believe in your ability to shape your reality, you will discover that this world is natural and waiting for you.

The moment to act is now. Trust in yourself. The world you've always envisioned is within reach. All it takes is your decision to step forward.

72

CHAPTER IX

The Link Between Health and Success

Health and success are deeply interconnected. Without a healthy body and mind, achieving a level of focus, energy, and creativity is nearly impossible to thrive in your work or personal endeavors. Conversely, achieving success can profoundly impact your health, fostering a sense of purpose, confidence, and well-being. Now, perhaps, is the right moment to examine the relationship between the two and explore practical examples of using thought forms effectively—both for your physical health and overall success.

Before we delve into specific examples, I want to clarify that the examples I'm about to give are not meant as **prescriptions**. We must learn to create our own thought forms tailored to our unique situations and desires. These examples will clarify fundamental principles and guide beginners, but ultimately, the thought forms you create must come from within.

Let's start by revisiting the example from an earlier chapter about the man who sold his house. If you recall, he listed the property with real estate agents but also formed a clear, well-defined mental image of the home being sold and of himself moving out. This simple but precise thought form worked for him. The house was sold, and his vision came to life.

What would have been the wrong way to go about this process? One of the worst things he could have done would be to imagine a specific buyer purchasing the house. This would violate one of the core rules of using thought forms: **never specify the person, time, or method by which your desire should manifest**. The Universal Mind knows far better than we do how to make things happen. Our job is to focus on the **what**, not the **how**.

He could have also created a thought form that included moving into a new home after the sale. While this wouldn't have been terrible, it would have been too indirect and distant from the immediate goal. The most effective approach is to focus on the primary desire—in this case, selling the house. Adding extra layers of complexity dilutes the energy of the thought-form.

The Danger of Over-Specification

This brings us to an important principle: specificity can either work for you or against you. On the one hand, a clear, well-defined thought form is essential. But on the other hand, being too specific—focusing on particular details like exact people, places, or methods—can block the natural flow of the Universal Mind.

Most people try to solve their problems in a very **objective** way. They make lists, tell their friends, post ads, network, and so on, hoping these external efforts will bring the desired results. There's nothing inherently wrong with these methods, and they often do work. However, using a thought form—working **internally**—creates a stronger and more consistent pathway to success. The objective world is essential, but the **subjective** world—the inner mental landscape where your thoughts, desires, and emotions reside—holds the real power.

When you focus on creating thought forms, don't worry if you can't articulate every detail right away. The Universal Mind will understand the essence of what you're asking for, even if your thought form isn't perfectly framed. Often, when people struggle to define their desires, they're unclear about what they truly want. Clarity is critical, and if your desire is still fuzzy, take some time to reflect before forming your thoughts.

Thought Forms Beyond Wealth: A Broader Perspective

It's easy to get caught up in the pursuit of material wealth. Money is a means of freedom, comfort, and security. However, focusing too much on wealth as an **end** often leads to dissatisfaction. We've all heard stories of people who amass great fortunes only to feel emptier than before. When it becomes the sole objective, wealth often becomes a burden rather than a blessing.

Over the years, I've heard countless people say, "Once I have enough money, I'll devote myself to helping others. I'll start a charity, give back to my community, or spend time on humanitarian work." Yet, many of these people—despite achieving financial success—never reach a point where they feel they have "enough" to fulfill their promises. They keep chasing more, and in doing so, they lose sight of their original intent.

That's why I urge you to **reframe your approach to thought forms**. Rather than focusing solely on acquiring wealth, think about what kind of work you truly want to do and what brings you joy and fulfillment. Imagine yourself in that role, contributing to society in a meaningful way. The money and material wealth will follow naturally when you're aligned with your passion and purpose. The **best plan for any thought form** is to see yourself engaged in work that excites and energizes you without worrying about the specifics of how the financial aspects will work out.

The Universe operates on its own timetable and through its own channels. By trying to control every aspect of the process—deciding how, when, or through whom your desire should manifest—you're **blocking** the Universal Mind from doing its job. Focus on **what** you want, and trust that the **how** will be taken care of. This requires faith, but it's a crucial part of the process.

Thought Forms and Spiritual Harmony

At this point, you might feel a bit overwhelmed by all the details, especially if you're beginning to explore thought forms. If you ever struggle, return to the **teachings of the Nazarene Master**, as they offer profound simplicity and wisdom. In those teachings, you'll find peace, rest, and a deep understanding of the Universe's natural laws. The path to success lies in aligning yourself with these **great laws of nature** designed to promote harmony, abundance, and fulfillment.

Whenever you find yourself straying from these principles, stop. Take a moment to reflect on your thoughts. Are they **constructive** or **destructive?** Are they aligned with the greater good? Are you operating from a place of fear, scarcity, or impatience? If so, pause until your inner guide tells you you've returned to the right path. Remember, **as your thoughts are, so will your results be.**

Discordant thoughts lead to discordant actions and results.

The Importance of Wealth Consciousness

One of the most significant shifts you can make is to stop thinking about poverty or scarcity, regardless of your current financial situation. If you're struggling financially, it's easy to fall into the trap of focusing on what you lack. However, this only reinforces those feelings of **lack**, keeping you stuck in a cycle of scarcity.

Instead, consider yourself wealthy in all the essential ways—**wealthy in health, spirit, resilience, and opportunities**. Wealth isn't just about money; it's about feeling rich in life, relationships, experiences, and your ability to contribute to the world. Many financially poor people are rich in spirit and will eventually rise above their circumstances. And conversely, many financially rich people are poor in spirit, their wealth serving as a temporary cushion that cannot fill the void inside.

The genuinely wealthy—whether rich or poor in material terms—recognize the abundance in life. They appreciate the beauty of a sunset, the power of music, the joy of nature, and the connection with others. Spiritual **wealth** attracts physical abundance because it aligns with the **Law of Attraction**. When you feel abundant, you attract more abundance into your life.

The Relationship Between Health and Thought Forms

Just as thought forms can help you achieve financial and personal success, they can also play a crucial role in maintaining and improving your **health**. Your subjective mind—the part of your mind that operates below the level of conscious awareness—is directly responsible for your body's vital functions. It controls digestion, circulation, nerve function, immune response, and countless other processes without your conscious involvement.

But here's the key: now that you know how to consciously control your subjective mind using thought forms, you can **profoundly influence your health**. Improved health is one of the quickest and most direct results you can achieve with thought forms.

Creating Thought Forms for Health

When using thought forms for health, the first step is eliminating **any thoughts of illness or disease**. Don't focus on a specific ailment, like imagining your weak heart getting stronger or your chronic pain disappearing. Instead, visualize yourself as a **healthy, vibrant, energetic individual**. Picture yourself doing the things you currently struggle with—activities that healthy people your age can easily do.

Your thought form should represent yourself as healthy, whole, and vital. See yourself as someone who radiates energy, strength, and wellness. The key is not to deny your current health problems but to focus on the positive outcome you want to achieve. The Universal Mind can only work through you to the extent that you allow it, and the more you focus on health rather than illness, the more your body will respond.

Streams of health and vitality flow through the universe, and they will flow into you once you've created a strong, positive thought-form for health. But it all starts with your **mental attitude**. You must stop thinking of yourself as sick or weak and start seeing yourself as strong, healthy, and full of life.

For example, if you want to gain weight, visualize yourself at your ideal weight, eat healthy foods, and feel energetic. If you're going to lose weight, imagine yourself slim, fit, and active without compromising your health in any way. The key is to visualize yourself **as you wish to be** without focusing on the negative aspects of your current condition. This allows the Universal Mind to work on your behalf, channeling the necessary energies into your body to make the desired changes. Remember, you are a part of the **infinite power of the Universe**, and this power will manifest through you to the degree that you allow it.

The Power of the Mind in Health

Even modern medical science recognizes the power of the mind in maintaining good health. Today, doctors frequently acknowledge the role of a person's mindset in their recovery from illness. The concept of the **"placebo effect"** is well-known. Patients who believe they receive effective treatment often improve, even if it has no medicinal properties. This illustrates the powerful connection between mind and body.

In many cases, the best doctors use less medicine and more **psychological reinforcement**, encouraging patients to adopt a positive attitude toward their recovery. They understand that a patient's mental state—their **will to health**—is one of the most critical factors in determining the outcome of their treatment. What a doctor can do for you, you can do for yourself through the power of thought forms.

This doesn't mean that medicine or surgery is unnecessary in severe cases, but it does mean that you can complement any medical treatment with the power of your mind. When you align your thoughts with the **positive flow of the Universe**, you set the stage for healing to occur more quickly and effectively. In this way, the objective mind can directly influence the subjective **mind**, which holds the image of perfect health.

Eliminating Illness from the Mind

Once you've created a strong thought form for health, it's essential to maintain it consistently. It would be best if you worked on eliminating **negative thoughts of illness** from your mind. This doesn't mean denying the reality of your current physical condition— if you're sick, it's natural to acknowledge that fact. However, dwelling on illness, pain, or discomfort can create a **self-reinforcing cycle**. The more you focus on what's wrong, the more your subjective mind absorbs those images, making it harder to break free from the cycle of illness.

Instead, focus on visualizing the **end result** of your healing journey. What will your life look like when you're fully healthy? How will you feel? What activities will you be able to enjoy again? Imagine yourself engaging in these activities with ease and joy.

This sends a powerful message to your subjective mind, telling it to align your body's processes with the vision of health you've created.

For example, if you're dealing with chronic fatigue, picture yourself waking up every morning with a sense of vitality and excitement for the day ahead. Visualize yourself going through your daily routine without feeling drained. As you repeatedly impress these images on your mind, your body will begin to respond, channeling the energy you need to overcome the condition.

Health as the Foundation of Success

In many ways, **health is the foundation** of success. You can approach your work with greater focus and enthusiasm when you feel strong and energized. Health allows you to pursue your goals with resilience, creativity, and determination. Conversely, when your health is compromised, it can be difficult to muster the energy needed to progress in your career, relationships, or personal growth.

Consider the example of high-performing athletes or entrepreneurs. Their physical health is often a top priority, and they recognize that maintaining their bodies allows them to operate at their best. For them, success isn't just about achieving goals—it's about having the **physical and mental stamina** to continue pursuing new heights of achievement.

But you don't need to be a world-class athlete or CEO to recognize the importance of health in your own life. Whatever your definition of success may be, it is rooted in your ability to show up every day with the energy, focus, and well-being to make things happen. This is why creating a thought form for health should be one of your priorities, even if your primary focus is on career, relationships, or financial success. Health and success are deeply interconnected; when you nurture one, the other often follows.

Thought Forms in Action: The Key to Long-Term Health

One of the most powerful ways to ensure **long-term health** is to adopt a mindset of **continuous self-care**. Thought forms are not just a one-time effort but a way of life. Each day, reaffirm your mental images of health, energy, and vitality. See yourself aging gracefully, with your body remaining strong and resilient well into your later years. Imagine your immune system working efficiently to protect you from illness and your mind staying sharp and clear.

In doing so, you are protecting your current health and setting the stage for a **lifetime of well-being**. The more consistently you use thought forms for health, the more deeply you will ingrain these positive images into your subconscious mind. Over time, they will become a natural part of your thought process, effortlessly guiding your body toward optimal health.

Avoiding the Trap of Negative Thought Forms

One of the most common mistakes people make is allowing **negative thought forms** to take root. We often don't realize how powerful our negative thoughts can be. Just as a positive thought form can bring health, vitality, and success, a negative one can create the opposite: illness, fatigue, and failure.

When you worry about your health and constantly think about how tired or sick you feel, you are, in essence, creating a thought form that reinforces those negative experiences. The more you focus on what's wrong, the more your mind and body will align with that negative reality.

The good news is that you have the power to **reverse this process**. By consciously focusing on positive, life-affirming thought forms, you can begin to undo the effects of negative thinking. It takes time, effort, and consistency, but the results are worth it. Remember, your mind is a powerful tool, and the thoughts you choose to focus on will ultimately shape your reality.

A Final Word on Health and Success

Health and success are not separate entities—they are intertwined. Without a foundation of good health, achieving long-term success in any area of life becomes a challenge. But when you use thought forms to focus on health, you create a solid foundation to pursue your goals with energy, clarity, and resilience.

Success, in its truest sense, is about **balance**. It's about creating a life where health, happiness, and purpose come together. By consciously using thought forms to nurture your body and mind, you set yourself on a path to lasting success—not just in your career or finances but in every area of life.

Remember, **you are a channel** for the Universal Mind, and you have access to unlimited power through this connection. Whether seeking to improve your health, succeed in your work, or live a more fulfilling life, thought forms are the key. Use them wisely, with intention, and watch as the Universal Mind works through you to bring your desires into reality.

CHAPTER X

Transforming Your Vocation into Your Vacation

Today, finding meaningful work—or the absence of it—seems to be a pressing concern for so many. With global shifts in economies, industries evolving, and societal expectations changing, the modern individual often struggles to find a balance between necessity and purpose. But can you consciously **create** your ideal job or career using the power of thought forms? Can you move beyond seeing work as a simple means to an end and transform it into a **vocation** that aligns with your deeper values and passions?

Let me start by sharing a true story illustrating how thought forms can play a pivotal role in shaping one's career. A while ago, a man found himself unemployed. For most of his life, he had enjoyed a steady stream of jobs that required little effort to secure. He had lived comfortably and had grown complacent. However, after a prolonged period without work, with his savings dwindling, he became desperate. It wasn't until this point that he realized he was doing what many others do—waiting for opportunities to come to him, aimlessly wandering from place to place, submitting applications, but lacking any true sense of direction.

Suddenly, it dawned on him that he had been neglecting the power he already knew he possessed. He knew the concept of thought forms but hadn't applied them in this context. The question was, **how** could he use them effectively in his quest for employment?

He focused on an office where he believed he had a good chance of being hired. He had worked there before and was familiar with the tasks he could perform. He visualized himself sitting at a specific desk, completing tasks he knew the company needed. He even pictured himself receiving a paycheck, feeling that sense of accomplishment and financial stability. He put all his mental energy into this image, impressing it deeply on the Universal Mind.

And it worked. He got the job.

But here's where things went wrong. His success was short-lived, and soon after being hired, he was let go. What had he missed? What flaw in his thought form had led to only temporary success? If you look closely, you'll see it: **he had focused too narrowly on a specific job in a specific office**. His mind created a temporary situation that aligned with his belief, but it wasn't a sustainable reality. He wasn't truly needed there, and no matter how powerful his thought form was, it couldn't override that fundamental fact.

So, what should he have done instead? The answer is simple yet profound. He should have envisioned **the type of work he wanted** rather than attaching it to a particular job or location. Instead of seeing himself in a specific office, he should have visualized himself in a position where he could use his talents, provide meaningful service to his community, and receive appropriate compensation. By focusing on the essence of employment—service—and letting the details work themselves out, he would have allowed the Universal Mind to guide him to the right opportunity.

The Essence of Employment: Service

What is the true nature of employment, anyway? At its core, employment is about service. It's about contributing to society in a way that aligns with your abilities, passions, and purpose. In today's world, the word "service" may seem overused, even clichéd, but it remains an honorable and noble concept.

When you approach your career from the perspective of service, everything changes. Instead of asking, "What can I get from this job?" the question becomes, "How can I contribute? How can I be of value?" When you align your intentions with this higher purpose and impress that desire on the Universal Mind, opportunities for meaningful work will appear. It may not happen in the way you expect or as quickly as you would like, but it will happen.

Returning to our story, he reflected on his mistake after the man lost his job. He realized that he had limited himself by focusing too narrowly on one position. So, he began working on a new thought form—a more general one. He visualized himself providing service utilizing his skills but without attaching himself to a specific company or role. Shortly thereafter, a friend approached him with an unexpected opportunity that perfectly aligned with his talents. Not only was the job fulfilling, but his salary eventually doubled.

What Not to Do When Creating Thought Forms for Employment

Now that you understand how to use thought forms to transform your career let's explore the **common pitfalls** you must avoid. The process may seem simple, but critical missteps can derail your efforts.

1. **Never imagine replacing someone in their job**. This is important. When you create thought forms that involve taking someone else's position, you introduce a negative element that undermines the very essence of the process. Thought forms should never harm others or be based on lack. The Universal Mind operates on abundance, and everyone always has enough opportunity.

2. **Avoid being overly specific about the type of work you want.** There may be opportunities you haven't yet considered, jobs that are far better suited to your talents than what you have in mind. By limiting your thought forms to a narrow set of possibilities, you may overlook something far more significant. Visualize the service you want to provide and the impact you want to make, and let the Universal Mind find the proper role for you.

3. **Don't set rigid time limits** for when the job must come. While it's natural to want a quick solution, especially when you're in financial need, remember that the best opportunities often take time to develop. Trust that the right job will come at the right moment, and have the patience to wait for it.

4. **Don't visualize getting money through deception or unethical means**. Any thought form that involves harming others or acting dishonestly will backfire. The Universal Mind supports constructive and positive actions that benefit everyone involved. Visualize yourself earning money in a way that brings value to others and makes you proud.

5.   **Don't picture yourself hoarding the results of your work**. There is more than enough for everyone. When you imagine yourself receiving wealth or success, also picture how to use that success to help others. Whether it's through charitable actions, creating new opportunities, or simply spreading positivity, align your thought forms with the principle of abundance.

Moving Beyond Fear: The Key to Success

One of the most significant obstacles to manifesting your desires through thought forms is fear. Fear can quickly undermine the process, creating a mental block that disrupts energy flow from the Universal Mind. Many people enthusiastically begin the visualization process, but doubt soon creeps in. "Can it be this simple?" they wonder. "Will this work for me?" These doubts are the seeds of fear and are fatal to your thought forms' success.

Shakespeare captured this perfectly when he wrote, "Our doubts are traitors and make us lose the good we oft might win by fearing to attempt."

There's a story about a traveler who encountered Death on the outskirts of a city. The traveler asked, "Where are you going, Death?"

"I'm going to the city to kill 30,000 people," Death replied.

A few days later, when the traveler returned to the city, he found that 100,000 people had died. Furious, he sought out Death and demanded, "You told me you were going to kill 30,000 people, but 100,000 have died! Why did you lie?"

Death calmly replied, "I only killed 30,000. **Fear and doubt killed the rest.**"

Fear is often more deadly than the circumstances we fear. It's estimated that most things we worry about—around 80%—never actually happen. Yet, the energy we put into fear can create the conditions we try to avoid.

Closer to home, there's the story of a preacher from Southern California who let a venomous rattlesnake bite him during a sermon. Most people would have sought medical attention immediately, but this man placed his faith in a higher power and fully recovered. He later said, "At no time did I lose my faith; I trusted that the Lord would help me."

While I wouldn't recommend letting rattlesnakes bite you to test your faith, this story illustrates belief's profound role in overcoming fear. Whether in a higher power or the Universal Mind, faith can be a powerful antidote to fear. And its faith that will keep your thought forms strong and effective.

Conquering Fear Through Thought Forms

Before you can expect to succeed in creating a fulfilling career, you must first conquer your own fear. And this is one of the first and most important applications of thought forms.

Create a mental image of yourself doing what you fear most: asking for a raise, starting a new business, or taking a risk in your career. Visualize yourself acting with courage, confidence, and positivity. You will shift your internal state by repeatedly impressing this image on your mind, replacing fear with confidence. Even with all the tools they need to succeed, many people are held back by a deep fear of failure, criticism, competition, or what others might think. These fears lead to feelings of inadequacy and ultimately sabotage their efforts. Remember, no person is an island. When you create thought forms, you are affecting not only your mind but also the minds of others.

Conquering Fear Through Thought Forms

Remember, no person is an island. When you create thought forms, you are not just affecting your mind but also the minds of others. The Universal Mind, by its very nature, is interconnected. When you impress a thought form onto it, you tap into a collective consciousness connecting all people. Your thought forms will ripple outward, making subtle impressions on the subjective minds of those around you. This is why it's crucial to create constructive thought forms—those that benefit you and the wider community.

The Power of Unity and Brotherhood

The interconnectivity of minds gives power to the idea of **human brotherhood**. We are all connected; what we think and feel inevitably affects others. This realization underscores the importance of aligning your thought forms with **positive intentions**. When you create thought forms that seek not only your own success but the success of others, you are contributing to the collective well-being. This is the essence of **true success**—when your personal growth helps uplift those around you.

Let's take a moment to reflect on what this means for you and your career. The job you seek, the vocation you desire, is not just about earning a paycheck or achieving personal fulfillment. It's about **how you can serve**. It's about how your unique talents and abilities can contribute to the greater good. When you focus on creating thought forms that align with this higher purpose, the Universal Mind will work in your favor, bringing opportunities that are satisfying to you and beneficial to the world around you.

This brings us to an important point: thought forms infused with love and service will always work for your most significant benefit. They will align with the universe's natural laws, and their manifestation will bring joy, fulfillment, and prosperity—not just for you but for everyone your work touches.

Faith vs. Fear: The Ultimate Choice

As you work with thought forms, you'll find that your journey ultimately comes down to choosing between two forces: **faith or fear**. These two emotions are mutually exclusive. You cannot hold faith and fear in your heart simultaneously. Where one exists, the other cannot thrive. This is why it's so critical to eliminate all doubts and worries before you begin creating your thought forms.

Many people begin with high hopes, but when doubt creeps in, they sabotage their efforts. It's easy to let the rational mind take over and question the effectiveness of thought forms. "Can this really work?" they ask. "Is it possible that my thoughts can profoundly change my life?"

These doubts are natural, but they are also dangerous. Doubt weakens the power of your thought forms, diluting their effectiveness and delaying their manifestation. When doubt takes hold, it's essential to stop, reset, and **begin again**. You must return to the start and reaffirm your faith in the process. Only when you are fully aligned with belief—without reservation—can your thought forms take root and grow into reality.

This is why it's important to build **mental resilience**. When fear or doubt arises, don't let it take control. Acknowledge it, but then consciously choose to return to faith. Strengthen your belief by focusing on previous successes or the stories of others who have successfully used thought forms. Remember the law: **"Ask, and you shall receive; seek, and you shall find."**

The Spiritual Foundation of Thought Forms

At the deepest level, thought forms are not just a mental or emotional exercise but a **spiritual practice**. By creating and impressing thought forms, you are engaging with the **Universal Mind** on a spiritual level. This is why it's crucial to approach thought forms with reverence and respect. The Universal Mind is not a tool for selfish gain; it is a sacred force that responds to purity of intent.

The ancient wisdom found in religious texts and spiritual teachings aligns with this principle. Consider the words of Jesus: "And all things, whatsoever ye shall ask in prayer, believing, ye shall receive." The key word here is "believing." True belief—faith without doubt—is the foundation upon which all thought forms must be built. When you align your thought forms with a **higher purpose**, the Universal Mind will respond by providing opportunities, resources, and guidance beyond what you might have imagined. The process becomes a co-creative act between you and the universe. You no longer work alone but in harmony with the creative force governing everything.

Practical Application: How to Create Thought Forms for a Vocation

Let's return to the practical side of things. How can you effectively create thought forms that will transform your career from a mere job into a **vocation** that brings meaning, purpose, and service into your life?

Here's a step-by-step guide:

1. **Clarify Your Vision**: Before you begin, reflect on what you truly want from your career. Focus not on specific job titles or roles but on the **essence** of the work you want to do. What kind of service do you want to provide? How do you want to impact the world? Your thought-form must be rooted in a clear and well-defined intention.

2. **Visualize in Detail**: Once you have clarity on your desired outcome, begin visualizing it in as much detail as possible. Picture yourself working in an environment where you feel fulfilled and surrounded by people who support and value your contribution. See yourself providing a service that brings joy to others and imagine the sense of accomplishment you will feel. The clearer and more vivid your mental image, your thought form will be more powerful.

3. **Infuse Your Thought Form with Emotion**: Emotions are the fuel that powers thought forms. As you visualize, feel the emotions associated with your desired outcome. Feel the satisfaction, the pride, the joy of contributing to something meaningful. The stronger your emotional connection to your thought form, the faster it will manifest.

4. **Release Attachment to Specifics**: While it's important to visualize in detail, it's equally important to avoid becoming too attached to specific outcomes. Let go of rigid ideas about the exact job or company you want to work for. Trust that the Universal Mind will guide you to the right opportunity, even if it's something you hadn't initially considered.

5. **Act with Confidence**: After you've impressed your thought form on the Universal Mind, act as though your

desired outcome is already in motion. Take steps in the physical world that align with your vision. Apply for jobs, network with others, and improve your skills—all with the belief that your thought form is actively working on your behalf.

6.   **Practice Patience and Trust**: Finally, be patient. Trust that the Universal Mind is working in its own time and in its own way. Don't rush the process or become discouraged if results don't appear immediately. Have faith that your thought form will manifest when the conditions are right.

Closing Thoughts: Transforming Work into a Vocation

Ultimately, transforming your work into a vocation is about much more than simply landing a job. It's about creating a life of **meaning, purpose, and service**. When you align your desires with the greater good and approach your career from a place of love and contribution, you tap into the full power of the Universal Mind. Your work becomes not just a means of survival but a pathway to personal growth and spiritual fulfillment.

As you move forward, remember that the most successful thought forms are those that align with **faith, love, and service**. They are grounded in the belief that you are here not just to take from the world, but to give something valuable in return. When you approach your career from this perspective, you will find that opportunities for success, fulfillment, and abundance flow naturally to you.

Now that you understand how to use thought forms to transform your work into a vocation, it's time to put these principles into practice. Begin creating your thought forms today and watch as your reality shifts to align with your highest vision.

The Universal Mind is ready to support you. The question is: **Are you prepared to use it?**

CHAPTER XI

The Energy Behind Your Thoughts

We've explored the foundational concepts of thought forms—how they shape your reality, work within the vast matrix of the Universal Mind, and guarantee results when applied correctly. The process might seem deceptively simple, but its power is profound. Once you master it, your life will change in ways you might never have thought possible.

However, there's more to this story than simply using thought forms for yourself. One of the most empowering realizations you can come to is that you can direct this force not just for personal gain but for the betterment of others. Imagine harnessing the energy behind your thoughts to improve your life and uplift and transform the lives of those around you. Doing this doesn't just create change in their world—you deepen your connection to the Universal Mind and enhance your journey. This interchange is one of the universe's greatest secrets: the more you give, **the more you receive.**

Helping Others with Thought Forms

Using thought forms to help others is both an art and a responsibility. It's tempting to think we know what's best for the people around us, but we must always approach this practice carefully. What we think is "best" for someone might not align with their actual needs, desires, or life path. There's an essential distinction between **forcing your will on others** and **offering them the tools to help themselves**. The latter is always the safer, more ethical approach.

For example, imagine a close friend is struggling with their health. With the best of intentions, you could create a thought form in your mind of them as vibrant, healthy, and full of energy. While this seems noble, ensuring that your desires do not drive this thought form for them but by genuinely understanding their wishes is essential. Always ask yourself: **Am I creating this thought form for their benefit or mine?** It's a subtle but vital difference.

One of the safest ways to help others with thought forms is by guiding them to create their own. This empowers them to take control of their destiny, aligning their mind with the Universal Mind. You can teach them how to visualize their goals, create mental images that reflect their deepest desires, and impress these images upon the Universal Mind. This process requires emotional engagement—a passion and commitment that only they can bring to their own thought forms.

The Principle of Teaching Others to Help Themselves

We've all heard the saying, "Give a man a fish, and he'll eat for a day; teach him how to fish, and he'll eat for a lifetime." This principle perfectly applies to the use of thought forms. Teaching others to harness this power gives them a lifetime of potential to shape their world. Thought forms are not a one-time solution; they are a tool for ongoing creation, allowing individuals to evolve and continuously bring new desires to life.

Think of yourself as a guide, not a savior. By explaining the visualization process and helping others understand the power of focused thought, you're empowering them to connect with the same universal mind you've tapped into. They learn they are not victims of circumstance but active creators of their reality. This shift in mindset is transformative.

Consider the profound change that occurs when a person realizes they have the power to improve their own life. The sense of liberation, confidence, and purpose that arises from this realization is immeasurable. People stop blaming external factors for their situations when they take charge of their thoughts. Instead, they focus inward, realizing that mastering their thoughts and emotions is the key to changing their world.

The Universal Mind and Its Role in Creation

What exactly is the Universal Mind? To fully grasp the power of thought forms, you must understand the nature of this vast, creative force that underpins all of existence. The Universal Mind is the infinite intelligence that permeates everything. It is not a distant, cold force but a deeply loving nurturing presence that seeks to express itself through all life forms.

Just as a river flows through the land, nourishing all it touches, the Universal Mind flows through you, through me, through every living being, constantly offering the energy needed to create, evolve, and expand. The more you align your thoughts with this flow, the more efficiently your desires will manifest. The Universal Mind operates on love—a creative force that wants growth, expansion, and harmony.

Now, imagine if you could consciously tap into this flow and direct it toward your goals. That's exactly what happens when you use thought forms. You become a channel for the Universal Mind's energy, guiding it toward your desired outcomes. But here's the key: **the more your desires align with the greater good, the more powerful your thought forms become**.

This is why selfless thought forms, created to benefit others or align with a higher purpose, often manifest faster and more comprehensively than purely self-serving desires. When your goals support the greater harmony of the universe, the Universal Mind works even harder to help you achieve them. It's as if you've tapped into a special reserve of creative power for those seeking to uplift others.

The Law of Reciprocity

The concept of reciprocity is not just a moral principle; it's a fundamental law of the universe. You cannot give without receiving, and you cannot receive without giving. The two are inextricably linked, forming a continuous cosmic energy cycle. When you use thought forms to help others, you are contributing to this flow. You are giving of yourself—your time, energy, and love—and in return, the universe responds by giving back to you. This might come in the form of material wealth, opportunities, relationships, or simply a deep sense of fulfillment and peace. The more you give, the more you receive because the universe recognizes and rewards those who contribute to the greater good.

But be careful: this law works in both directions. If you hoard your energy, talents, or resources, you block the flow, and the universe responds accordingly. Just as a dammed river eventually stagnates, so does the life of someone who refuses to share their gifts with the world. The more you withhold, the more you cut yourself off from the abundance the universe constantly offers.

A powerful story illustrates this principle. Imagine a man who amasses a fortune through great effort and persistence. At first, he's generous, sharing his wealth with those around him, contributing to his community, and enjoying the fruits of his labor. But over time, fear creeps in. He becomes afraid of losing what he has, so he starts to hoard his wealth, refusing to share it or invest it in anything that doesn't benefit him. He builds walls around his fortune, both literally and figuratively.

What happens next? His wealth begins to decay. He invests in things that don't prosper, his relationships deteriorate, and he becomes increasingly isolated and miserable. The more he holds on to his wealth, the more it slips through his fingers. This story illustrates a simple truth: **wealth, like all forms of energy, must be in constant motion to remain vibrant and alive**.

The same applies to your thought forms. When you use them generously—when you create them not just for yourself but for the benefit of others—you set into motion a cycle of abundance that will return to you in ways you might never have imagined.

Aligning with the Universal Mind

One of the most important concepts to grasp when working with thought forms is the idea of **alignment**. It's not enough to visualize what you want and hope for the best. Your desires must align with the Universal Mind's greater purpose. This means that your thought forms should benefit you and contribute to the harmony and well-being of others.

Think of it this way: the Universal Mind is like a vast orchestra, with every living being playing their part in a grand symphony of creation. When your thought forms are in harmony with this symphony, they resonate with the universe, and your desires are easily fulfilled. But when your thought forms are out of sync—driven purely by selfish motives—they create discord, and the universe resists.

This is why it's so important to approach thought forms from a **spiritual perspective**. You are not just creating a mental picture of what you want; you are engaging in a creative act that involves the entire universe. Your thought forms must be rooted in love, compassion, and a desire to contribute to the greater good.

Practical Steps for Using Thought Forms

Now that you understand the more profound principles behind thought forms let's talk about how to use them effectively. Here are some practical steps to get you started:

1. **Clarify Your Intentions**: Clarify your intentions before creating a thought form. Ask yourself: is this desire in alignment with the greater good? Will it benefit others as well as myself? The more transparent and selfless your intentions, the more powerful your thought form will be.

2. **Visualize with Emotion**: Thought forms are powered by emotion. When you visualize your desired outcome, don't just see it in your mind—**feel it**. Imagine the joy, satisfaction, and gratitude you'll experience when your desire becomes reality. Emotion gives energy to your thoughts, making them more magnetic to the Universal Mind. Without emotion, your thought forms will lack the vitality they need to manifest.

3. **Focus Consistently**: One of the key factors in successful thought forms is **consistency**. Don't let your mind waver between conflicting desires. Pick one or two clear goals and focus on them with unwavering attention. This means regularly revisiting and reinforcing your visualizations with the same emotional energy. The more often and intensely you focus on a thought form, the more quickly it will manifest. Think of this as "watering the seed" of your desire so it can grow into full bloom.

4. **Align with the Greater Good**: As discussed, alignment with the Universal Mind is crucial. Before you even begin visualizing, take a moment to offer your thought forms to serve the greater good. You might say, "May this thought form benefit me and those around me. Let it contribute to the harmony and well-being of all." This simple intention sets the stage for your desires to be fulfilled in a way that resonates with the universe's natural order.

5. **Act Upon Your Thought Forms**: Visualization alone is not enough. You must take concrete steps toward your goals. The Universal Mind rewards action. When you create a thought form, you're planting a seed, but you must also cultivate the soil by taking action in the physical world. If your thought form involves improving your health, make healthier daily choices. If it involves financial success, take practical steps toward improving your skills or seeking new opportunities. Thought forms don't eliminate the need for action; they **enhance** and **amplify** the results of your actions.

6. **Be Open to Receiving**: Often, people block their progress by not being open to receiving the fruits of their thought forms. This can happen in subtle ways. You might think you're ready for success, but deep down, you could harbor doubts or feelings of unworthiness. It's essential to **let go** of these limiting beliefs. Open yourself up to receiving what you've visualized, and trust that the universe will provide when the time is right. Let go of the **how** and focus on the **what**—the details of how your thought form manifests are the universe's responsibility, not yours.

7. **Practice Gratitude**: Gratitude is one of the most powerful emotions you can cultivate. When you feel gratitude, you are in a state of receiving.

By thanking the universe in advance for fulfilling your desire, you align yourself with the energy of abundance. Practice gratitude daily, not just for what you already have but also for what's coming to you. This reinforces your thought form and signals to the universe that you are ready to receive.

The Spiritual Dimension of Thought Forms

It's important to recognize that thought forms are not just about achieving material success or fulfilling personal desires. They are part of a much larger spiritual process that connects you to the **Universal Mind**. This connection is sacred. It reminds you that you are a co-creator with the universe, constantly shaping reality through your thoughts, actions, and intentions.

When you create thought forms with this awareness, you are not just manifesting objects or experiences—you are contributing to the evolution of the collective consciousness. Every positive thought form you create helps to raise the planet's vibrational frequency, bringing more love, harmony, and abundance into the world.

Many people approach the practice of thought forms with the mindset of "What can I get?" But the true power of thought forms is unlocked when you ask, **"What can I give?"** How can your thought forms serve the greater good? How can they contribute to the well-being of others? When you approach thought forms from this perspective, you'll find that your desires manifest more quickly and experience a deeper sense of fulfillment and purpose.

Tapping Into Cosmic Intelligence

One of the most exciting aspects of working with thought forms is the realization that you are tapping into **cosmic intelligence**. The Universal Mind is an infinite source of wisdom, creativity, and knowledge. When you align your mind with the Universal Mind, you access this cosmic intelligence reservoir. This is why thought forms often bring solutions and opportunities you might not have imagined or considered alone.

For example, you might create a thought form for career success and find that the universe brings you a completely unexpected job opportunity—one that is even better suited to your talents and desires than you could have planned for. This is the magic of thought forms: they allow you to co-create with the universe, which has a much broader perspective than your individual mind can comprehend. Trust in this intelligence and allow it to guide your thought forms to their highest potential.

A Final Word on Responsibility

With great power comes great responsibility. Thought forms are powerful tools, but they must be used with integrity and care. Always ask yourself: Is this thought form aligned with the highest good? Am I using this power responsibly, not just for my own benefit but for the benefit of others?

When you create thought forms with love, compassion, and a desire to serve, you become a channel for the Universal Mind's energy. This energy will flow through you, bringing abundance, joy, and fulfillment—not just for you but for everyone you touch. The more you use thought forms in service to the greater good, the more powerful they become, and the more you align yourself with the creative forces of the universe.

So, what will you create? What thought forms will you bring into the world? Remember: **your thoughts have energy and power, and your thoughts have the potential to shape not only your own life but the lives of others.**

Now that you understand the energy behind your thoughts, you must use this knowledge wisely. Whether creating thought forms for yourself or helping others do the same, always align your intentions with love, service, and the greater good. In doing so, you will not only achieve your personal goals but also contribute to the ongoing evolution of the universe itself.

A Heartfelt Farewell: Embracing Your Journey Forward

As we reach the final words of this journey together, I want to take a moment to express my deepest gratitude for allowing me to be a part of your transformative experience. This book has been more than just words on a page; it has been a shared voyage—a co-creation of energy, intention, and possibility.

Throughout these pages, you've been invited to explore the depths of your consciousness, to challenge the limits of what you believed possible, and to step boldly into the role of the creator of your own reality. It has been a journey of discovery, empowerment, and profound inner growth. And now, as you prepare to close this book, know that the journey doesn't end here; it is only just beginning.

Life is a wondrous, ever-unfolding adventure, and you are the architect of its design. Every thought you nurture, every emotion you embrace, and every action you take shapes the reality you live in. You hold within you the power to create a life that resonates with the deepest desires of your soul—a life filled with love, joy, abundance, and peace.

But as you move forward, remember that the path of conscious creation is not always linear. There will be moments of doubt, challenges that test your resolve, and times when the road ahead may seem unclear. In those moments, return to the truths you've uncovered here. Remember that you are never alone; you are always connected to the infinite wisdom of the Universe, and you possess all the tools you need to navigate whatever comes your way.

It is also essential to hold space for yourself with compassion and patience. Transformation is not a destination; it is a lifelong journey of becoming. Honor each step you take, no matter how small, and celebrate the growth from every experience. Trust in the process and be guided by the gentle whisper of your intuition, the spark of inspiration that lights your path.

As you continue your journey, may you carry with you the knowledge that you are a powerful creator, capable of manifesting your dreams and shaping your destiny. May you find the courage to follow your heart, the wisdom to learn from every experience, and the strength to rise above any obstacle.

Most importantly, it would be best to remember to live in alignment with your highest truth. Let your actions be guided by love, integrity, and a deep sense of purpose. In doing so, you will not only create a life of fulfillment and joy for yourself but also contribute to humanity's collective awakening.

As I bid you farewell, know that my wish for you is one of infinite possibilities. May your journey be filled with light, love, and the realization of all you will become. The Universe is vast, and the potential within you is limitless. Embrace, trust, and let your life be a testament to the incredible power of conscious creation.

Thank you for walking this path with me. Though our time together on these pages is drawing to a close, your journey continues—one that I hope will be filled with endless wonder and boundless creation.

With all my love and deepest admiration and respect, Choyo Gomex

As We Conclude This Journey Together...

Here we are, at the end of **TRANSFORMATION**, a journey I hope has sparked something significant in your life. From the very first page, through every concept and exercise, you've allowed these ideas to enter your mind and heart—and for that, I am profoundly grateful.

How are you feeling after this journey? Have these ideas inspired or shifted something within you? I would love to hear about the moments that resonated most, any transformations you've experienced, or even the challenges you faced while integrating these concepts. **Your reflections are precious to me**, and I'd be honored to learn about your personal experience with the material.

Writing this book has been a labor of love and knowing that it has touched your life means more to me than words can express. But this isn't just my journey—it's yours, too. You've actively participated in this process, applying each idea to your own life. **Your insights, thoughts, and experiences matter. They have the power to influence not just this book** but also the lives of others who will embark on this same path.

So, if you feel called to share your thoughts, I'd be honored. **What stood out to you the most?** What new insights or transformations are you carrying forward? What would you like to see more of or explore more deeply in the future? Your feedback will help guide me as I continue to share this message with others, and your voice could be the key to helping other readers find their own breakthroughs.

From the bottom of my heart, **thank you** for joining me on this path of transformation. This book may have ended, but your journey is only just beginning. I look forward to hearing about where your path leads you next.

With all my gratitude and Respect,

Choyo Gomex

Congratulations On Completing The Reading Of TRANSFORMATION

The fact that you've made it this far shows that you are truly committed to transforming your financial life and reaching a new level of prosperity.

Completing a book is something few people achieve, and you've done it. That's phenomenal.

I am a **Master Practitioner of NLP, trained by Dr. Richard Bandler**, and as a token of my gratitude and to recognize your dedication, I am offering you a personalized **45-minute coaching session, completely free of charge**, via Zoom.

This is an opportunity for us to talk in-depth about your Master Plan to manifest your wealth and ensure you are on the right path. If you are interested, simply send me an email at: **choyo@gomex.com**, and we will coordinate a date and time that best suits you.

I am here to help you take the next big step towards your wealth and economic prosperity.

I'm already doing my part; now, it's your turn!

Suggested References for "Consciously Creating Your Reality"

1.   **James Allen** – *As a Man Thinketh* A timeless classic on how our thoughts shape our circumstances and outcomes in life.

2.   **Dr. Joe Dispenza** – *Breaking the Habit of Being Yourself: How to Lose Your Mind and Create a New One* Explores the intersection of quantum physics, neuroscience, and personal transformation.

3.   **Napoleon Hill** – *Think and Grow Rich* One of the most famous personal development books of all time, focusing on the power of thought and belief in attaining success.

4.   **Carol S. Dweck** – *Mindset: The New Psychology of Success* A deep dive into the fixed vs. growth mindset, and how adopting the latter can change your reality.

5.   **Eckhart Tolle** – *The Power of Now: A Guide to Spiritual Enlightenment* Focuses on the importance of present-moment awareness in transforming consciousness.

6.   **Neville Goddard** – *The Power of Awareness* Discusses the power of imagination and how one's awareness and self-concept directly shape their reality.

7.   **Maxwell Maltz** – *Psycho-Cybernetics* This foundational work explains how self-image influences behavior and outcomes, based on the principles of cybernetics and psychology.

8.   **Dr. Wayne W. Dyer** – *The Power of Intention: Learning to Co-create Your World Your Way* Discusses how we can align our intentions with the universal force to manifest change in our lives.

9.   **Louise Hay** – *You Can Heal Your Life* Explores the connection between mind and body and how our beliefs and thoughts impact physical health and well-being.

10.   **Shakti Gawain** – *Creative Visualization: Use the Power of Your Imagination to Create What You Want in Your Life*

A guide on how to use mental imagery to create the life you desire.

11. **Dr. Bruce Lipton** – *The Biology of Belief: Unleashing the Power of Consciousness, Matter, & Miracles* Explores the science behind how thoughts influence the physical world, particularly our health and biology.

ABOUT THE AUTHOR

Choyo was born in a poor little village named La Majagua in Michoacán, México. While working in the fields of his village he had dreams of better things and a desperate desire of improving his financial condition. He was intrigued by why some people are abundantly wealthy while most others barely have enough to survive, and was determined to figure out why.

Choyo Gomex has lived in California for over 35 years. For fifteen of those years he was an undocumented worker desperately looking for the road to success.

On May 1973, at the early age of 18, he left his hometown, and in the trunk of a car, he crossed the border into the U.S, risking his life in the pursuit of the "American Dream". Once in the U.S. Choyo was fortunate enough to have found one of the best trainers in self development of his time, Mr. Earl Nightingale, who coach him on how to be a successful individual.

His resolve of never taking "NO" as a final answer, and his unbreakable will to succeed, allowed him to enroll at Pepperdine

University where he graduated in 1986 with a Bachelor's Degree in Business Administration, – While still undocumented – and two years later graduated from National University with an MBA in Marketing.

His degree had a price tag of $120,000 at that time, which was an exorbitant amount considering he was earning only $1.75/hr as a dishwasher.

Choyo understood the importance of having a good education and never allowed a lack of money to become a roadblock to obtaining one. "You do not necessarily need to have money to get a good education," he says. His mentor taught him that he could Do, Have, or Be anything he wanted, that all he needed to succeed was a strong desire to achieve his goals, determination, and willingness to pay the price by doing things in a certain way.

Choyo finally found the key to success. He retired from work at age fifty and has written several books. Now, he is eager to share his formula for success with everyone who wishes to attain it. His audiences now have the opportunity to use what he has learned on his journey to achieving success for himself and his enterprises.

His keynotes show each person how they too can get started towards achieving any goals they truly desire.

For more information, please visit the website:
www.choyo.com